# WELSH F*****

A collection of thoughts and ideas from a guy whose life got changed by a language.

*O'r Gymraeg a fu i'r Gymraeg a fi.*

Stephen Owen Rule

Hunan-gyhoeddwyd gyda hawlfraint
© 2020 gan Stephen Rule

Cedwir pob hawl. Ni chaniateir ailgyhoeddi neu ddefnyddio unrhyw ran o'r llyfr hwn mewn unrhyw fodd heb ganiatâd perchennog yr hawlfraint ar wahân i ddyfyniadau mewn adolygiad llyfr.
Am ragor o wybodaeth, cyfeiriad: ste_cymru_14@hotmail.com.

Argraffiad llyfr cyntaf: Gorffennaf 2020
Argraffiad e-lyfr cyntaf: Awst 2020

ASIN B08DDH59FG (llyfr print)
ASIN B08DMLWCGZ (e-lyfr)

Dyluniwyd y clawr gan Stephen Rule

---

*Self published and copyrighted*
*© 2020 by Stephen Rule*

*All rights reserved. No part of this book may be reproduced or used in any manner without written permission of the copyright owner except for the use of quotations in a book review. For more information, address: ste_cymru_14@hotmail.com.*

*First paperback edition: July 2020*
*First ebook edition: August 2020*

*ASIN B08DDH59FG (paperback)*
*ASIN B08DMLWCGZ (ebook)*

*Cover design by Stephen Rule*

*I dedicate these words and ideas to my wife, Angharad, who, in addition to being the warmest, kindest, and most wonderful person I've ever met, was the last piece of the jigsaw in my acquisition of Welsh.*

# CYNNWYS

**PENNOD 1:**

**Cymraeg a Fi (Welsh and I)**

**PENNOD 2:**

**Addysgu'r Gymraeg (Teaching Welsh)**

**PENNOD 3:**

**Dysgu'r Iaith (Learning the Language)**

**PENNOD 4:**

**Pam lai'r ddwy? (Why not both?)**

**PENNOD 5:**

**Amddiffyn ein Cymraeg (Protecting our Welsh)**

**PENNOD 6:**

**Iaith Arbennig (A Special Language)**

# RHAGYMADRODD
## *Foreword*

For the past 10 years or so my desire to write a book has resided wholly in a few still-incomplete documents lost in the vast depths of my computer's cloud drive. One such project attempts to encourage learners of all six living Celtic languages (at the same time) to build simple sentences to gain at least a foothold in communication. I eventually envisage it as being a companion to people whose only outlet to use and to practise their Celtic language skills is on social media platforms. Decent idea or silly pipe dream? Either way, one day I'll get around to completing it.

I'm not a writer and would never claim to be. And yes, that is indeed a subtle encouragement to be patient with my words. My passion and, in truth, my only real ability lies in teaching languages. It was only recently that I entertained the audacity to believe that writing about what is essentially my own personal story would be of interest to anyone. While this book is in no way intended to be an autobiography of any sort, my hope is that my experiences and my journey towards fluency in the Welsh language will be of benefit to others wishing to take up the challenge of learning our native language themselves. I also hope that people who are already fluent (as a native or a former learner) and, in particular, those who teach the language as a vocation might also find some kind of wisdom in these pages.

*"To me, Welsh is the most beautiful music and every Welsh speaker is a musician. Listening to the language and speaking it every day is an indescribable joy. How I lived without it for 52 years I will never know, but to live without it now would be unthinkable. #CymraegAmByth"*
- @simonchandler50 via Twitter.

Beginning with a quotation from someone I've never met, probably never will meet and who I don't even follow on Twitter (shame on me) is, I suppose, the epitome of this book. I could have easily quoted Huw Edwards, Rhys Ifans, Ben Davies, John Saunders Lewis, Gwynfor Evans or even JRR Tolkien to help me express what the Welsh language means to me and to so many others around the world. I could have also chosen from a range of other famous quotations littered throughout history expressing what languages in general mean to their respective authors. This one just stood out to me and, just like how the random choosing of it epitomises this book, the words contained in it epitomise our language. Right, while you enjoy this book, I'm off to follow Mr Chandler on Twitter. Hope he follows me back!

# PENNOD 1
# CYMRAEG A FI – Welsh and I

## CYMRAEG O'R CRUD
*Welsh from the cradle*

I was brought up in a small village in Flintshire in the north east called Leeswood to a completely non-Welsh-speaking family in a completely non-Welsh-speaking area. All four welcome signs around the village read 'Leeswood' in English followed by a completely different variation of **Coed-llai** to each of the other three. One without a hyphen but two separate words, one without a hyphen with the two elements stuck together and one that capitalised the *LL* after the hyphen – something never done in Welsh. Simply by the fact that I 1) noticed this in the first place and 2) felt the need to share this information probably tells you more than enough about my often-pedantic nature.

The Welsh-language had come a long way (in the wrong way) in this former mining village; from residents in the mid-nineteenth century protesting a rule forbidding the language's use in the local colliery pits – and getting shot for it – to what we see today; ie no more than 15% of residents say they can speak Welsh. It's probably worth noting that, to my knowledge at least, 0% use it out in public. The language was just never passed on through the generations. It was seen as backwards and pointless. A drawback to progress. And that's how it remains.

My own initial interactions with the Welsh language in my early years were exactly as they should have been – totally oblivious to me. It's key to language acquisition, in my opinion. I've found that the more conscious one is of a language, the more one really must knuckle down to make it stick in the brain. I guess that's the reason behind youngsters being so susceptible to learning languages effectively on account of them being massively less susceptible to caring about why languages behave the way they do, and how they're perceived when speaking other languages. Progressing in age doesn't mean we can't progress in learning a language, but it does make us more aware of the process of learning and it hence often creates a psychological barrier between ourselves and our linguistic goal(s).

For instance, I didn't realise that the word *taid* wasn't just what everyone else on the planet called their grandfathers until I was around eight. Everyone else in my friendship circles either called their grandfathers *taid* or didn't bat an eyelid when I used the word around them. According to a census record I found when researching my family tree some ten years ago, my *taid* was listed as a Welsh speaker as a child – a fact I didn't learn until after he'd passed away shortly after the turn of the new millennium. I'd often hear him call the dog with **'tsyd o'ne!'**, he'd always mix up borrow/lend, way/road and learn/teach – a throwback to the fact the Welsh language doesn't differentiate between these terms – and when he was tired he'd often state: **'Dw i wedi blino rŵan. Dw i'n mynd i gysgu'** – *'I'm tired now. I'm going to sleep.'*

My youthful naïvety meant I never considered I was actually hearing two different languages. To me, these slightly odder-than-usual sounding words and phrases were just what everyone else in the world said. I'd begin writing my address with **4 Bryn Alun** and I attended **Ysgol Derwenfa**. Our teachers greeted us each morning with '**Bore da**' and we'd say '**Ga' i fynd i'r toiled, os gwelwch yn dda?**' when our little bladders were full. Again, I'd love to say as kids we all just accepted Welsh but, honestly, we didn't even notice it.

# CYMRAEG YN CYRRAEDD
*The arrival of Welsh*

My only ever dislike (if I can call it such) towards Welsh came between the ages of about 8 to 11 – coincidentally around the same time I first became conscious that 'other languages' existed and not everyone on the planet spoke what I spoke. The teacher who taught me Welsh in primary school did so in a wonderfully enthusiastic way and children clearly learned with her. Her and her husband – our headteacher – Doug Jones, were pivotal in ensuring Welsh was all around us in our school environment. There are phrases Mrs Jones taught us and lessons she delivered to us that I still remember to this day. **"Mae'n braf tu allan felly dydyn ni ddim angen y golau"** (*It's nice outside so we don't need the lights*). We were eco-friendly back then, too!

It truly was zero reflection on either of them that I just didn't like Welsh. The exercise books were just so different to other subjects and the lessons felt, through absolutely no fault of the school, as if they were just 'in the way'. Welsh felt like a chore and made me question why I needed two words for a *chair* and *rain* when the ones I already had worked just fine.

In my second year of high school at around 12 years old I quickly began to notice that Welsh was one of my stronger subjects – probably owing to the superior teaching I'd ungratefully received in primary school compared to the provision children from other primaries had received. The four ex-Ysgol Derwenfa crew in my high school Welsh classes just seemed to have a far greater grasp on Welsh than everyone else. I always gave my best in school, but Welsh lessons were, somehow, easier than others and, with a bit of extra thought, I found my skills were good enough to begin pushing my work further without needing to ask my teacher for additional tasks or help. Welsh just seemed to *work* in my head, but living in such an English-orientated area still made me ponder why I needed two ways of saying things when I was still getting on fine in my first 12-or-so years of life with just one for each. Even so, my enjoyment was growing.

Later on that academic year, my teacher explained to the class that there was an opportunity for some students to attend a Welsh-language sing-along session in another local school. To be brutally honest, the prospect of an afternoon off school was more appealing than singing in a funny language with what was likely to be 90% primary school-aged children but I, just like everyone else in the class, put my hand firmly up in the air to register my interest. Rolling her eyes and sensing we'd all worked out that the trip meant getting some time off school, the teacher informed us that only 3 students could go from our class. In the fairest way possible, she explained how next lesson she'd be handing out invitation letters to the top three students who'd shown an interest. The top three students... of which I was not one, as it turned out.

Most of the other kids groaned at the missed opportunity to sack off school for an afternoon and then they just got on with their lives – probably to never have it cross their minds again. In a way I wished I were more like them because I'd worked myself up into such an excitement that I truly believed I had a genuine chance of getting picked. Like I said, I wasn't overtly bothered about going or not, but I really thought I'd at least have been asked. I suppose my newfound, youthful arrogance probably needed nipping in the bud anyway.

But no, I wasn't just going to leave it there. I'd tried my best in class and had behaved well. I needed an explanation. The bell went for the end of the lesson and everyone left for break time. Now was my chance find out what I'd been doing wrong, but before I had the chance to embarrass myself and display nothing short of downright cheekiness, it was my teacher who spoke first.

"*You're my first reserve, Stephen*" she said without any prompting. "*Sorry, we only had three spaces. If anyone can't make it, you'll be getting an invitation.*" And that was good enough for me. I could leave with my head held high and my hopes of missing double Geography next Tuesday afternoon restored. The cynic in me, however, thought that she'd only said it to make me feel better and that she'd probably say the exact same thing to anyone else who might have come to her feeling disappointed. But such cynicism was short-lived as, a few days later, one of the lads who'd received one of the three golden tickets to the Welsh-singy-thing declared he was unable to go. True to her word, the teacher's invitation was mine.

I don't particularly remember much about the event and hence I don't believe that attending it was what first sparked my love for Welsh. I guess that must have been coming regardless. Perhaps it was that a teacher had kept her word and I truly was the fourth best in class. Result! Whatever it was, my life changed in the days and weeks that followed. I was going to learn Welsh.

# CYMRAEG AIL IAITH
## *Welsh second language*

When I was in school, Welsh was an optional subject for GCSE but, even though those who didn't opt for it still had to endure one solitary hour per week, it was the first subject on my GCSE options form. I also opted for German and French but was told I had to choose between them as three languages would be too much for me. I now know around eight languages to a decent degree of competency. Despite this fact, I still don't know the French word for *'irony'*! Probably because I chose GCSE German, I guess.

I loved GCSE Welsh. At the beginning of my second year of the course our teacher, with whom I'm still in touch, left for Patagonia in Argentina to teach the language out in the Welsh colony there. Even after losing such an inspirational figure my love for the language continued, so much so that I was beginning to converse in Welsh – however basic it was – to my teachers and peers in class. I was scribbling notes of any new words I'd hear in the lesson at the bottom of each page of my exercise books and I was browsing Welsh dictionaries for pleasure. Not quite your regular teenager, huh?! Don't get me wrong, I still played football after school with my mates and owned the latest games on my snazzy PlayStation 2 console, but Welsh was always at the forefront of my mind. I'd often get my mother, whose only Welsh knowledge genuinely is one swear word, to say the word for the huge things that grow in fields with bark and leaves just so that, when she inevitably said 'tree,'

I could giggle and tell her she'd just said the Welsh word for the number three. For the first time, having a second word for something excited me and, especially in my locality, something rather unique. A whole world untouched.

On the daily walk home after a game of football behind the village community centre with the lads, any moments where no one was speaking I would be 'commentating' on my own life in Welsh – in my head, of course. I wasn't a complete loser! "**Dw i'n cerdded lawr y stryt efo fy ffrindiau. Roedd pêl-droed yn hwyl heddiw.**" (*I'm walking down the street with my mates. Football was fun today*). It was the only practise I could get. If I didn't know a word in a sentence that I'd attempted to make, guess what the first thing I'd do when I got home was…

I was different. And because I was different, I quickly became aware that everyone had their own interests themselves. I also understood that Welsh might not have been part of other people's plans for their futures, but none of this deterred me more from the sadness I felt that others just weren't as keen on Welsh as I was. It just didn't make sense to me. The language lives in us – fluent or not – and we have a responsibility as those who call Wales their home to at least consider our linguistic inheritance and heritage. This, and the fact we held the potential to talk about other people behind their backs when they walked into the park – we weren't old enough to do it in pubs, of course.

When I'd ask them, it was always the same response from my mates. "*I don't like Welsh!*" "*There's no point!*" "*I just don't think it's fun!*" And how could I argue? Languages aren't easy and I've come to realise that they require nothing less than a total life change to get anywhere near fluency. From talking to yourself on the way home to forcing yourself to converse with real Welsh speakers whenever possible, I knew I was going to have to *live* in the language to truly learn it. Remove myself from my English-speaking comfort zone – something that most people, when given the chance, would rather not do. Once again, I struggled to blame anyone for not wishing to throw themselves into the fiery pits of potential linguistic embarrassment when, in all honesty, the fact they're fluent in English means they don't actually have to.

But you do have to. You have to change your life almost entirely in order to create opportunities that are often simply not there – especially with a minority language in an English-dominant area. It was on my friends' responses some 10 years prior that it was 'no fun' and 'pointless' that I based my teaching philosophy and continue to do so to this day. Yes, it takes a certain kind of person to be a teacher, but to be a *language* teacher I realised I'd have to tackle the things my friends disliked. I had to make Welsh fun and, perhaps more importantly, I had to show there's a point to learning it.

My A-levels were tough and as much as I loved History, Physics and Maths, their difficulty meant they were hardly enjoyable. Of course, learning about our past and our cosmos and our... erm... *algebra* all in one day was any young lad's dream for school, but the requirements of the qualifications meant lots of homework and lots of examinations. Welsh, however, was my release. In many ways it was my *reward* after a full day of equations and dates. An A-level subject I enjoyed so much that I didn't ever feel like I was falling behind or drowning in the amount of work that was being set. I was having fun making my own revision materials that my teachers ended up sharing with other students. It wasn't without its challenges, certainly. Discussing films and poetry through the medium of a language in which I wasn't yet fluent was a big ask, but I was understanding too much to not see light at the end of the tunnel.

It's also worth noting that, of the whopping 13 students who opted to take A Level Welsh in my year group, 6 of us were ex-students of Leeswood's Ysgol Derwenfa.

# GWRTHWYNEBWYR
*Rivalries*

Because I had expressed a desire to become a teacher, I was advised to visit a local school as part of my 6th form work experience. At 16, my love for Welsh was a secret to no one – especially the organisers of our work experience placements – and it was suggested that I use my work experience week to spend some time in my nearest Welsh-medium primary school – Ysgol Terrig. My Welsh-speaking bus driver told me she knew the buses that ran to Treuddyn from Leeswood and that she'd get me a place for the week. It's not what ya' know, right?

Treuddyn – Leeswood's rival village. There were always tales that some solid lad was looking for one of our lads or one of us was after someone from Treuddyn. Nothing ever actually happened, granted, but just the name of the place made us Leeswoodites sick to the core. On top of this, the fact them lot had one of the only Welsh-medium schools in the whole area made me dislike them more. To be fair, Treuddyn is quite famous in the world of Welsh culture; boasting a village Eisteddfod that has run since 1863 as well as the wonderful, little, village primary school known as Ysgol Terrig which feeds Mold's Ysgol Maes Garmon.

The week I spent there scared the hell out of me. The staff were wonderful, and the children were great, but I was a hugely anxious teenager and totally out of my depth. One occasion that will forever stay with me as the very first time I had a full-blown conversation in Welsh (with someone other than my Welsh teachers) was at a table of year 3 children. Okay, so all we talked about were the football teams we supported and our favourite colours but sitting at that tiny table surrounded by tiny chairs hosting tiny humans conversing freely in Welsh meant the whole world to me. I genuinely still remember the insane smile that adorned my face when I left to go and work with another class. Even though it meant that my A-level Welsh course had only delivered fluency to the same degree as a bunch of 7-year-olds, I didn't care one bit.

Speaking to the adults in the school was a different story entirely. I remember one teacher speak to me in Welsh at lightning pace rendering my understanding of her instruction at close to nil. Hoping to remain polite amidst an onslaught of nerves I nodded at her until a few seconds later she whispered in English; *"You don't understand a word of what I'm saying, do you?"* Looking back the teacher clearly meant no malice in her question but, on top of wishing the ground would swallow me up, my hopes of fluency took a decent battering in that moment. I've been back to that school a few times since becoming a teacher myself and it's only ever there I develop a temporary, yet unavoidable, arrogance about me that I'm now fluent and that such a memory can never haunt me again. Maybe it's because I go there representing *the 'Wood* and I like showing them Treuddyn lot that we speak Welsh too, but it only ever happens in that school.

I look back with huge gratitude at my week in Ysgol Terrig but, if I'm honest, I learnt absolutely nothing about classroom management or creating an engaging learning atmosphere.

Through no fault of their own, my tunnelled vision had eyes only for the Welsh language and how much of it I could soak up.

# RHUGL O'R DIWEDD
*Fluent at last*

I remember being told by friends and family that, upon my arrival in Aberystwyth as a student, I'd be a fluent Welsh speaker in three months. Being around a living language would train my brain to hear the sounds of Welsh and it would slip into my mind in no time. That did not happen. Three months turned out to be a whole year of squinting my eyes at lecturers somehow believing it would increase my understanding of the words coming out of their mouths. In the end, however, I got there and one day it just seemed to click. I'd turn on S4C and understand people. I'd pop Radio Cymru on and not stop once to tell myself "*Ooo, I understood that word, it means [whatever]!*" My head just got on with taking in information in another language. I still pause now and again and zone out of a report on Radio Cymru to remind myself how insane it is that I can simply understand it. But as great as it was to comprehend my new world, I couldn't shake the feeling that the language natives used so freely derived from a place from their childhood as they began to identify the world around them. Their words came with such ease and it made me rather jealous. Acquisition of language in early childhood can never be retrieved by someone who's gained fluency as an adult, even if they bring up their own children and get to watch all the cartoons on which they themselves missed out. I'm still bothered by this today, but I've managed to come to peace with the fact that said feeling is okay to possess, and it does not mean I should deny calling myself a fluent speaker.

University was incredible – and not just because of the 'social' side! It was the first place I was ever educated fully through the medium of Welsh and it was the first place I experienced social, spoken Welsh. On one occasion my friends and I were discussing something raised in the lecture while the lecturer was still talking. Naughty, naughty! Unfortunately for the lecturer, resulting in us getting told off with '**ishd yn y cefn**' (*hush at the back*). This was less of a threat to me and more a reason to be weirdly proud at being shouted at in Welsh for the very first time in my life at the humble age of nineteen.

There were tough times too. Throwing myself into the belly of the beast by choosing Neuadd Pantycelyn (Aberystwyth University's Welsh-speaking halls of residence) was nerve-wracking. My fellow students were chatting away in a mad concoction of pacy slang and unintelligible tags. One lad who showed us round sounded like he kept saying my name after everything he said... turns out he was just saying '**sti?**' – a tag much like the English *'ya' know?'* Another time there was a knock at my door and a lad I'd seen around the halls walked in and just threw words at me. Thankfully, a native speaker friend was with me and sorted out what he was asking for. Red football socks. That was literally it. I got worked up because someone asked to borrow some red football socks. But, like I said, perseverance prevailed... even if my inhibitions took a huge bashing.

Buying unhealthy amounts of books and snacks was doing nothing for my booze-fuelled social life so my dad suggested I look for a job while I was away at uni. My only previous job had been a paper round when I was about 14 which my dad had had to organise for me. Being cheeky enough to ask for work from random strangers wasn't in my anxious repertoire. When my uncle dropped me off at the start of my second year we visited a local hardware store for some supplies. We paid for the items and, without warning and clearly having spoken to my dad, my uncle asked if there were any jobs going. The owner took one look at me and probably thought that her excuse to let me down lightly was to ask "'**Dych chi'n siarad Cymraeg?**" I don't think "**Ydw**" was the response for which she was hoping. To be fair, she immediately asked for a copy of my lecture timetable. The next passage of events continues to make me chuckle at just how different dialects of Welsh can be. "**Dwi efo fo adre'**" (*I have it at home, lit. I'm with it at home*), I said. The reason behind her pause of a few awkward seconds only became clear to me a few days later when I realised that her dialect of Welsh would probably have expressed this as "**Ma' 'da fi fe gytre'**." Either way, from that moment on I was an employee of Ann Ellis of H & A R Ellis earning £5 an hour filling sacks of bird seed and cutting keys. Side note; how are there so many different types of keys? There's genuinely a whole book on it!

Over the years I interacted with so many locals around the Aberystwyth area; the lion's share of them Welsh speaking. I once served the then-mayoress of Aberystwyth, Sue Jones-Davies – the 'Welsh tart' of Monty Python fame. It was the farmers who intrigued me the most. Once I'd finally gotten to grips with their husky tones and slurred words (sorry, I'm a village boy), it made me giggle that, instead of thanking me with the conventional "**diolch yn fawr**," they'd all bid me "**Thanc iw, gw'boi**" (ie '*good boy*') as I presented them with their new keys and change.

On my last day working for Ann she told me how my Welsh had changed so drastically in those two years. She'd never really commented on my language until then and it showed me that, even in this world where Welsh was just the done thing, its use still brought its speakers pleasure. At the time I put my progress down to being around the language in lectures and friendship groups etc but, honestly, it was having to throw myself into actually speaking it with people day in day out until I simply had no time to congratulate myself for completing a conversation in Welsh because someone else was waiting to be served. It put me constantly on edge every day, but I learnt quickly that taking oneself out of one's comfort zone is an effective remedy for serial anxiety. I still pass the old shop when I go back to Aberystwyth. The place is closed and empty now, but the name still emblazons the panel above the door and the memories flood back and bring a smile to my face when I see it. All the best, Ann. Diolch yn fawr.

# FI ARALL
*Alter ego*

For so many young people and adults alike, the anxiety and potential for embarrassment when trying to unleash your Welsh on strangers is one that falls into the trap of simply being too easy to avoid. In my third year of the university, eight of us rented a house on Stryd y Thespis by the little Spar and the Cambria Vaults pub in the town – alumni will know where I mean. Four of the lads were first-language Welsh speakers and the rest of us had been reading the language as our degree. Despite the amount of Welsh we possessed, the language of the house was largely English – at least for the first term. Each of us fell into the trap of either not wanting to seem stupid in front of our mates by speaking broken Welsh, or not wanting to speak Welsh in case the others didn't understand. I'd love to say the reason we eventually changed our ways was the feeling of guilt in denying our national language but, honestly, we were usually too drunk to care.

Initially, the only time we'd really use our Welsh together was when other Welsh speakers were around. Visits from family members, mates coming for a beer and in the butchers where we'd regularly get a few steak because we spoke Welsh - maybe it is 'what you know,' after all? To be honest, we'd always end up fighting over the ninth steak so it probably wasn't worth it!

What changed the situation for me personally was inspired by interactions with those local, deep-voiced farmers asking me to cut their keys. Their Welsh was littered with inaccuracies, missed mutations and English words lobbed in now and again which showed me that Welsh is so much more than a formal language resigned only to literature and history. So, instead of being 'myself' and not wanting to feel embarrassed using my less-than-perfect language skills, I created an alter ego for speaking the language to my housemates. Whenever I spoke Welsh I'd lower my voice to a husky drone, chuck '"**na fe**" at the end of every sentence and pretended to be a 50-year-old, post-mid-life-crisis, valleys gentleman who'd worked the coal pits since birth. Whenever I made a mistake, it was my alter ego who did it, not me. Now I'm not advocating everyone take on stereotypical southern valleys accents to speak Welsh and I realise I'm probably a psychiatrist's dream case, but if you've got Welsh-speaking mates and fancy a laugh, it worked for me. We still occasionally drop in the accent when we catch up these days for a laugh. Might be an idea to explain your intentions prior to trying it, mind. Don't need no people in white coats being called on your behalf.

# IAITH FI, IAITH PAWB
*My language, everyone's language*

By the end of university my goal was complete. My aim was to become fluent in Welsh by any means necessary – getting a degree out of it was just a bonus. My last piece of work, a dissertation about the state of the Welsh dialect of my home county of Clwyd, was the final cherry on top of my fluent cake.
It was a pleasure to work on. It also meant I had a new passion to pursue now that there wasn't much else I could learn about the Welsh language's history, struggles, successes and ever-evolving battle to maintain its relevancy in a world so brutal to languages that stand still. My dissertation research took me places in my own patch of which I'd never heard before, as well as meeting incredible people with even more incredible stories of unique and peculiar terminology used in the area. It was hugely interesting to see how, even only 150 years ago, the Welsh language was thriving here. One man from Ffynongroyw in northern Flintshire told me that, even until around 60 years ago, **Sa'sneg** (*English*) was referred to as '**iaith cŵn a chathod**' to most residents – *the language of the cats and dogs*; explaining how English would only be used to order animals about. At the time I found it both funny and heart-breaking that I would always speak English at home and at school but would practise my Welsh on my cats – a total opposite from when Welsh lived.
Looking back, the most notable thing about my university days was learning languages like Irish, Breton and Scots Gaelic

through the medium of Welsh. Psychologically, with so much new terminology and so many new phrases being thrown at me in languages of which I'd never even heard a few years earlier, I was clinging to the Welsh I knew to ensure I understood and kept up with my lectures. It threatened on many occasions to force me into a feeling of 'I can't do this' but, having stuck with it and persevered, I believe it was this reliance on the Welsh I had that forced my brain to attain the language quicker. I've recently taken on a pre-GCSE French class in my school and, as well as being a nice change from constantly teaching Wales' beautiful language, squeezing in any opportunities to teach French through the medium of Welsh has been a really interesting experience. Seeing my students subconsciously accept Welsh as their 'base language' to decipher another has been really cool. If you ever fancy giving this tactic a try yourself, Say Something in Welsh offers a Spanish course through the medium of Welsh that'd keep you on your toes. Other than that, you'll have to wait until I finish my *'Manx Gaelic for the Welsh speaker'* book.

By the end of my time in the university, I began replacing the word 'learner' with 'speaker' and it felt great. I remain, however, under no illusions that the journeys of others to learning Welsh (or learning any language…. or learning any*thing*) are never the same. I was aware immediately that my story of losing my **'dysgwr'** tag was a unique one and I'm glad I was wise enough to appreciate this fact from an early stage.

# SYLFAEN FY MYD
## *Welsh rocks!*

Rupert Soskin, an amateur archaeologist (amongst many other things) specialising in the largely forgotten Neolithic and Bronze Age monuments of the British Isles, once described the challenges faced in understanding our ancient history as follows; *"Imagine it snows and somebody builds a snowman in the time-honoured way of a lovely carrot for his nose and two lumps of coal for his eyes. And then the warmer weather comes and the snowman melts. Then one day you're walking across the field and you come across the two lumps of coal and the carrot, but you have no knowledge of the tradition of making snowmen. What would be your interpretation? A messy coal man with a careless donkey? But then worse still, say, a sheep came along first and ate the carrot and you're excavating the lumps of coal thousands of years later. That's the problem with our distant past; fragmented pieces from different jigsaw puzzles and we just don't know what goes with what. It's a nightmare, but it's so exciting."*

Even after the admittance of fluency, the Welsh language still felt a bit like this to me. My road to fluency was run but I couldn't shake the feeling in my gut that there was still more travelling to do. Every time I closed one door another opened, sometimes two or more at once. Nothing quite humbles a person like the realisation that there's always something more to learn and explore – even if the prospect of true understanding might never be realised. Along the way there had been occasions when Welsh came easy to me and days I felt I'd gone backwards. I still get the latter now, but a lot less frequently, **diolch byth**!

Speaking my nation's native language opened up so much about the land where I first saw daylight than I ever imagined possible, from its history to its modern day and beyond. I began to imagine a Wales in which I wanted to live. Beyond any doubt, this land has so much to offer the world. I hope it will always be a place that keeps a welcome in the hillside for those returning home and taking up learning its language, as well as keeping the same welcome to those starting out to make Wales their new home. With so many people from nations far and wide choosing to make their homes here whilst maintaining their own native languages, both speakers and learners of Welsh are opening their eyes to how best *they* can ensure their own language is also maintained and it's bloody wonderful.

# PENNOD 2
# ADDYSGU'R GYMRAEG – Teaching Welsh

## BREUDDWYD DOD YN WIR
*A dream come true*

I always wanted to go to university and I always wanted to become a teacher, but had you asked me from an early age what I wanted to read in university and, subsequently, what I wished to teach as a teacher, I'd have said History. History doesn't just offer a chance for students to acquire analysis skills; it gives teachers a chance to teach their classes about facts and events from their own nation that, owing to a lack of any kind of Welsh media, would cease to have ever existed in the hearts and minds of ordinary people. My only problem? I simply wanted to be fluent in Welsh more than anything. Welsh continued to call to me during my GCSEs and A-levels but swathes of grammar (plus the ability to analyse an 80-year-old poem) wasn't going to be enough. On top of this, my enjoyment in the subject compared to most other students whispered to me that I should teach Welsh. I felt I understood concepts in unique ways and was able to articulate tough grammatical concepts effectively when my mates asked for help. If I could make it fun and show there's a place for it in modern society, perhaps I could encourage more young minds to take up the challenge.

After I qualified as a teacher, my philosophies shaped my style. In addition to understanding that the vast and various needs of every learner are incredibly diverse, the old moans of my own school friends continued to ring in my mind. *Make it fun and show them it's useful*. I like to think I have done and continue to do that.

But it's not all flowers and sunshine. Teaching hormonal teenagers who insist they often know better can be tough – no matter your subject. As the years went on, it was the smaller things that put a smile on my face and pushed me to keep improving as a professional – even when it seemed that my work wasn't always appreciated. I remember a particularly tough lesson with an *interesting* class of year 9 students last lesson on a Friday afternoon. Full of lunch time sugar and excited for the weekend…. the graveyard shift. I was still learning my trade back then and I'm not ashamed to admit that it was a tough lesson. The hour beforehand I'd had a super-enthusiastic first-year class who were like little language-sponges. The contrast with the class that faced me next that afternoon could not have been more obvious. I looked back on what we'd achieved after they'd hurriedly left the room at 3:30pm and all I could think of that I was confident they'd taken from the lesson was one solitary, new word: **ansbaradigaethus** (*amazing, incredible*). Ironically not an adjective I'd have used to describe the lesson itself. I beat myself up all weekend until that Sunday evening when I realised that no matter how bad that lesson was, every one of those students left with a little bit more Welsh than they walked in with. I did that. It became obvious to me in that moment that no amount of admin and no amount of sugary excitement was ever enough to prevent at least some Welsh filtering through. Nevertheless, I still asked my colleagues for advice. I couldn't let a lesson like that happen again. One idea put forward was to make sure my lessons with that class had plenty of short, snappy tasks to keep them on their toes. And it worked. It worked so well that I began using the technique with other classes. Success. Was this the key?

As it turned out, not quite. Not all classes were a sugared-up nightmare, but I was using tactics as if they were. It took me another year or so to realise that students also liked free reign when using Welsh. Just because one technique worked, didn't mean I shouldn't be varying with my styles. One lesson, for example, after a previous lesson of short, fast-paced vocabulary acquisition, I set a task and presented my success criteria. "**Ysgrifennwch**! *Just write*," I implored. Students asked for a lot of words that day and my pedometer was as tired as I was by the end, but the students worked. 30 minutes of writing in a different language. It was almost as if they enjoyed that element too. They felt confident with the words they knew and, more than anything, enjoyed mixing and matching with existing and newly acquired terminology. They were creating new synapses; new connections in their minds. Every word or phrase they asked me for offered me an opportunity to give the class a mini lesson just around that idea. It was awesome.

Not only had my dream of getting the chance to teach young people Welsh (and getting paid for it) come true, but I felt I was breaking new grounds in the quest to make Welsh come to life. Students who just loved languages for the hell of it (like I used to be) were not going to come around too often – my own high school years taught me that. I tried my best to be fresh and I believed it was working. I questioned how far I could take it.

# RHOWCH FODFEDD; CYMERANT FILLTIR
*Give them an inch; they take a mile*

Most teachers cover their classroom walls with students' work. I, however, am far too lazy to be exchanging letters and paragraphs around every academic year only to look back and not recall a single student stop and spend five minutes of their fifty-minute lunchtime reading about some random 11-year-old's trip to Abersoch for the weekend. Honestly, I wasn't surprised. Initially I used to feel rather harsh on my students, most of whom produced genuinely amazing work that was more than good enough for a place on my walls. I justified my laziness by completely re-thinking how I used my wall space. Okay, so trading up students' work for permanent displays was hardly revolutionary, but noticing how the more words that were on display the less students paid attention to them got me thinking about efficiency and how, whether we're young or old, we're far more likely to pay attention to bitesize chunks of information rather than any huge swathes of it. It's probably why social media is so popular.

And so, what if every time I introduced a new way of starting a phrase there was a bank of verbs (often the lifeblood of a sentence) on my wall so that students could simply say what they wanted to say? Around my walls over the next few weeks I took down my year 7s' essays (I did apologise to them and bribed them to not be sad by feeding them Jaffa Cakes – they were fine about it after that!) and replaced them with a whole wall of verbs. Useful ones like *'speak,' 'watch,' 'play'* and *'eat'* mixed in with some rather obscure ones like *'explode,'* *'download'* and *'fight'*. Three verbs per A4 laminated page – Welsh verb in bold above the English translation below in italics. Despite the Welsh words being above their English translations, I organised the whole lot into alphabetical order according to the English – for example my first poster reads '**gallu** – *able (to)*, **ateb** – *answer*, **gofyn** – *ask*) – making it easier for students who were, 99% of the time, translating from English to Welsh in their minds. Finally, I coloured all the A words in blue; the Bs in orange; the Cs in yellow, etc. My wall became a huge, colourful dictionary of verbs and, after taking the time to teach my students how and when to use the wall, they've never looked back since. Actually, seeing as said wall is at the back of my classroom, technically they have looked back quite a bit, but you get the point!

The proof was in the pudding. I remember introducing '**Bydda i'n**' (*I will / I will be*) to some year 8 students and, just before we packed away for the end of the lesson, I told them to make any sentence – the funnier the better – in their heads by popping a verb after **Bydda i'n**. I told them it would be cool if they could add even more words to their sentences after the verbs, but it wasn't essential. Some of the stronger students were making sentences like '*I will explore the field*' and '*I will not display a poster in my bedroom.*' Sentences for which we'd struggle to ever find use in everyday life – no matter what language we speak – but it made them giggle and they felt good that they were able to do it. It was the not-so-strong students that impressed me most though. No, there wasn't too much extending past adding a verb to '*I will*' but the giggles were incredible. *I will explode. I will fight with Spiderman. I will download FIFA today.* No leash restricting them to give me fifteen different ways of telling me they like eating pasta and what they like on the radio, but an open stage to shout out sentences they'd never heard before and would probably never hear again or, at times, sentences that showed off their new games or what they'd bought on the weekend. They were doing it in Welsh.

Later I hung an A3 poster from the roof that read '**Mae \_\_\_ yn = \_\_\_ is.**' Forgetting that most Welsh sentences begin with the verb (English tends to prefer the subject) was a big problem across all ages so having something I could just tap with my board pen when I read a sentence like '**Mr Rule yn hoffi pêl-droed**' – this sentence should begin with *mae* – made life so much easier for me and began to sink into students' heads rather quickly. I broke up the remaining space on my walls with some gimmicky memes about the Welsh language and a few easily translatable jokes and tried my best to make my classroom a celebration of the language the students already possessed. At the same time, it gave them the tools to unlock more of my wall space as their journeys towards Welsh competency progressed; "*What's that meme mean, sir?*" "*You'll be able to work it out by year 9.*"

Many adults ask me how much grammar is involved in teaching Welsh these days – probably looking for comparisons with their own experiences of learning the language at school. Looking back on my journey some 20 years ago, there did seem to be much more parrot-fashion, go-home-and-learn-these tasks. Tattered textbooks filled with tables of funnily spelt words and verb tables galore with a guaranteed phallic shape somewhere on every other page. My own personal collection of various language-learning books includes a few of them (verb tables, I mean. Not penises) and I admit, even into my 30s with a huge passion for languages, I still avoid them as much as I can. And I genuinely love grammar too! Grammar is important but it's something that falls into place naturally when the language is freed of its shackles.

As language teachers, often our first battle is sparking an interest in the language so sending students home to read and re-read 10 words they'd scribbled unwillingly into their books at the end of their last lesson was not going to spark a great affection – as much as one can understand and accept the reason behind it. Going home to a choice between trying to learn 10 words in WELSH or playing the latest game on their phone in ENGLISH.... this was no longer just a teachers' problem. Subconsciously it was destroying Welsh. Students making subtle choices in their mind that the language of pleasure was English and the language of sit-down-and-learn was Welsh.

Teachers often despair at the timeless cliché of 'give them an inch and they'll take a mile.' Let them whisper to their friends whilst working and within five minutes they'll be shouting across the room. Let them use their Welsh dictionary apps on their mobile phones in class and two minutes later they're watching a video someone shared on social media of a puppy rolling off a sofa. But we can command this cliché as our own.

Give them a simple sentence and let them loose with it. Give them the tools to say what they want. Let them say stupid things and let them use you [the teacher] as the punch bag – the amount of times I've heard that *'Mr Rule is a loser'* and *'Wrexham AFC are rubbish'* is beyond me but I absolutely love it. After all, they're hardly wrong!

## GORAU ARF ARF DYSG, 'DYDY?
*The best weapon is education, right?*

Seeing so much pleasure and passion in the students when they were afforded free reign outlined something to me; we all want success straight away. Every January I go back to my gym religiously 3 or 4 times a week. By February it's back down to once per fortnight (if I'm lucky!) because I'd lost faith that I was making any progress. Feeling like we've wasted our time is a killer for most things – none more so than language learning. We want to be shown that even five minutes of hard language studying can show results. This fact is the same, if not worse in many ways, for students too. Their progression needs to be made explicit to them in order for teachers to expect them to maintain their interest. One of the first pieces of homework I ever set as a fresh-faced, twenty-two-year-old teacher was for my year 7 group to open their books when they got home, read what they'd done in the lesson that day and simply be proud of what they'd achieved. No writing, no researching, and no extra learning. I wanted them to see that one small lesson can produce wondrous results.

But, as Irish language activist and former Education Minister in Ireland, Eóin Mac Néill once said; "*There can be no greater delusion than to imagine that a language can be kept alive alone by teaching. A language can have no real life unless it lives in the lives of the people.*" This quotation has stayed with me as an ever-existing reminder to keep my feet on the ground and to ensure that I impart my love of Welsh on the students as well as my knowledge of it. It emphasises the weight of the task in hand and humbly reminds me that we, as teachers, can't do it alone. It also exemplifies somewhat of a concern in me that the perhaps the weight of such a heavy task as defending a language can weigh heavy when solely placed on the shoulders of young people alone.

Despite this cynical yet understandable notion, speaking to the many people who received their education through English but who also possess a great respect and love for the Welsh language (whether they're fluent or not), the story of the inspiring teacher came up repeatedly. No matter their *alma mater* and no matter their location in Wales, many former teachers' names are readily recalled even decades after leaving school. In a handful of cases, contact between people and their former teachers was maintained. In my own case, Melvina Roach, Pauline Maxwell and Clare Vaughan, my Welsh teachers during my mid-teens – have become friends of mine since leaving school as well as friendships with inspiring lecturers such as Dr Ian Hughes and Dr Rhisiart Hincks, whose passions ensured my love for Welsh (and all languages), are maintained after my years in the university. More importantly than any of the Welsh they ever taught me, they showed me that it's the ways and methods we employ to teach languages to school children (and beyond) that's the key. Get it right, and young people are hooked; get it wrong and they're lost forever – unless they find their own way back in later life.

Teaching Welsh is always on my mind. Sometimes, I'll just be quietly sitting and I'll conjure up an obscure way to potentially teach a certain concept, or even just a word. If that's what it takes to inspire students, I'm more than happy to carry the burden of never switching off. Teaching languages, much like teaching anything, is nothing short of a sacrifice on the part of the educator. How often will teachers see students who excel in their subject go on to claim hugely successful careers in their field, all the time knowing that the knowledge they worked so hard to possess (and later impart) has led others to realise dreams the teachers themselves could so quite easily have pursued? It's bordering on arrogant to consider, but coming to peace with this fact and, of course, being immensely proud of our students' life achievements that is the true measure of a successful educator.

## PWY SY' AR FAI?
### *Who's to blame?*

It's certainly no secret that teachers often face the brunt of blame regarding the current vitality of Welsh. Neither is it a secret that the Welsh language was in far better health 150 years ago than it is today. Avoiding the socio-cultural reasons behind its decline, there's no time like the present to look forward to how we can reverse Wales' language shift. For this, there's no better place to start than with a sister-language of Welsh, Scottish Gaelic. A report in 2020 about the future of Gaelic yielded some damning forecasts and sparked a huge surge in people worried about the fate of Scotland's ancient tongue spoken by less than 60,000 people in the country. The report condemned the language to certain death by the end of the decade, and speakers and academics alike took to airing their concerns.

Dr Cassie Smith-Christmas of Ollscoil Luimnigh (*The University of Limerick*) wrote for the popular Scottish blog, Bella Caledonia, in the July of 2020 under the headline *'A Child Eye's View of Language Revitalisation: Hope and opportunity for the future of Gaelic in Scotland.'* In her piece, Dr Smith-Christmas explained how only on rare occasions did only *"one particular factor [...] explain why children may or may not speak a particular language"* recognising that multiple factors were at play when it came to languages dying with older generations.

Exploring the reasons behind language death, she writes, *"It would be tempting from this basic info to simplify and say, 'It must be something the caregivers are doing 'wrong" or that 'The school isn't enough.' My work over the years has shown me that there is very rarely - if ever - one particular factor to explain why children may or may not speak a particular language. Families do not exist in vacuums after all and speaking the language to the child is only ever half the battle. Children after all have their own agency and are influenced by a myriad of factors both internal and external to the family. Thus, despite overcoming many obstacles, Gaelic language use in this family continues to be an uphill struggle."*

Despite her point clearly outlining issues with how efficiently and successfully schooling is utilised that simply cannot be ignored when attempting to revitalise a struggling language, my own thinking was immediately brought to occasions where children being pulled out of Welsh-medium education because parents believe their child is struggling. Witnessing this first-hand as a teacher in an English-medium school who, every year will see at least two or three young people move from Welsh-medium education into my school is truly heart-breaking. This isn't to say that educators don't acknowledge and understand parents' concerns, but pinning the blame on Welsh-medium schooling is often a stark misplacement of blame. On many occasions, a child's former struggles in academic subjects continue after changing the language of education, leaving them only excelling in Welsh as a second language. As Dr Smith-Christmas makes perfectly clear, hoisting the vitality and preservation on the already overloaded shoulders of young people and expecting results is, frankly, unfair; *"Things that may seem trivial to us as adults can make a significant impact on the relationship the child has with Gaelic and thus, the more the child positively experiences her or his world through Gaelic, the more likely he or she is to use the language."*

The finger of blame often falls on the educators where, in truth, a whole host of cultural and social reasons are hidden behind the scenes. Dr Smith-Christmas' article proves how whether or not we are willing to adapt our own culture to make a home for struggling languages will eventually lead to whether we still hear them as living modes of communication. Dr Smith-Christmas references a resilience I've always known to be the key in encouraging Welsh to flourish once again. She recognises how we, as passionate *learners* of today, may end up being the necessary link between a language living or dying that eventually yields the passionate *speakers* of tomorrow. Whatever our reason for learning Welsh, we must accept this position and work with it.

# WASTAD YN DDYSGWR
*Always a learner*

Any teacher will tell you that admin and bureaucracy regularly get in the way of what we love to do best – teaching. We know it can't be avoided and we understand the thought process behind doing it all, but if I used every hour I've spent on admin on instead planning lessons and creating inspirational resources, perhaps grades would be even better than we currently achieve.

It became obvious to me that, for whatever reason and whether I liked it or not, expecting all students to leave school at 16 as competent Welsh speakers was just not realistic. Yes, they could hold a simple conversation and discuss the weather but not much else. Even most of the stuff we learn for examinations is trivial. We'd genuinely acquire more language reading Welsh books for 6-year-olds and singing nursery rhymes… really! For me it's the most frustrating truth about teaching this language. I'm not moaning – how many students leave fluent in French or German after school for example? But a couple of hours per week simply aren't enough. No student can live in a language (ie the prerequisite to becoming fluent according to Mac Néill's quotation in the previous section) via two lessons per week.

Over in Ireland there are similar concerns with the teaching of their native language in English-medium schools. In 2008, American-born, Irish comedian Des Bishop decided to spend one year in the Irish *Gaeltacht* (areas where Irish use outweighs English in everyday life) with the intention of performing a comedy set completely in Irish at the end. The series, entitled *In the Name of the Fada* (*Fada* being the name for the acute accent (´) found on many Irish words that elongates vowels; much like the circumflex (^) does in Welsh), is a heart-warming 5-part series aired on Irish-language channel TG4 of how throwing oneself into a language – however 'niche' – can produce amazingly successful results. The whole series can be found on YouTube these days and is well worth the watch. Aside from its jokes and light-hearted, feel-good nature, the series highlights several important recommendations on how to improve Irish provision on the island; not least regarding the teaching of the language in English-medium schools. It's reckoned that the Junior Cert qualification in *'basic'* Irish can be achieved in 1,200 hours of teaching. The next level, *'middle,'* requires 2,100 hours, while the *'advanced'* level demands some 5,000 hours to achieve. Time that is easier afforded in principle than it is in practice. In fairness, the Junior Cert syllabus is as well thought out as our new Welsh GCSE syllabus but the admin boxes and assessment targets on both sides of Saint George's Channel still means it can fall short of realising its real purpose of actually producing fluent speakers. They're seen by many teachers to offer too many opportunities for short cuts and a temptation to anticipate examination questions, hoisting pupils over the grade thresholds but leaving them with a less-than-extensive learning experience.

We're always learners – even when we think the job's done. I'll read books in my native English on my e-reader device and am always glad of the fact I can simply tap a word to find its definition. This might not be enough to make me question my fluency in English, but it's humbling enough to make me realise that learning is an ongoing, life-time process. It's reckoned that one must use a word 72 times to make it stick in the brain. With an additional language, that number is much higher. Couple this with the fact there are obviously thousands of words in the Welsh language and that old motivator '**dal ati**' (*keep at it*) becomes a mindset that learners of all ages simply have to adopt.

Even after reading Welsh in the university and then later making regular visits to Welsh-speaking areas to associate myself with a whole host of Welsh speakers elsewhere, something I read about Irish learner Michael McCaughan in his book entitled *'Coming Home: One man's return to the Irish Language'* really struck a chord with me: *"You are always a learner. That's why you say "Tá Gaeilge agam", I have [some] Irish, but not "Tá an Ghaeilge agam" [I have [all of] the Irish] — you never have the whole of the language."* In Welsh, the equivalent of this phrase is "**Mae Cymraeg gen i**" - *There is [some] Welsh with me*.

Being humbly modest and open to admission that anyone and everyone is far from perfect is, in my opinion, one of the best traits teachers and speakers alike can possess. It requires practice and a lot of effort but I can promise you, as someone who does it day in day out, it's not only your students' grades that will see the benefit of such modesty, it's the entire Welsh language.

# BETH YDY 'AIL IAITH'?
*What is 'Second Language'?*

If you received your education through English in Wales, chances are you're probably aware of the term 'second language.' Thankfully, the term itself is being deleted in modern education in Wales, but it will take perhaps a generation or more to dispel its legacy. Aside from it creating an aura of Welsh being a 'second rate' and, ultimately, a less useful skill to possess, nowadays, with more and more young people able to already speak multiple languages before even embarking on acquisition of Welsh, the term certainly needs to become obsolete as soon as possible.

Despite a national desire for change, I've been less than impressed, however, with some of the campaigns against this outdated system of learning. It isn't too long ago that members of the pressure group Cymdeithas yr Iaith (*The Welsh Language Society*) pulled a stunt at the National Eisteddfod in 2015 where lead campaigner Jamie Bevan climbed atop a battered Peugeot 205's roof and proclaimed that teaching Welsh as a second language is "a total write-off beyond repair" and was nothing more than a "failed educational experiment." As a learner whose skills had come via the system, it was hard to see the stunt as anything other than gimmickry; potentially angering the small numbers of Welsh people who had acquired their Welsh via this system and making them feel like the language they possessed was of a lesser standard. Either way, the new curriculum is on the horizon in Wales [at the time of writing] and we all hope a more efficient and dignified dawn awaits the language's provision for young people.

But, for many, the damage has already been done. Coupled with not-so-fond memories of parrot-fashion learning, poor teaching, or simply an insecurity amongst young people that languages are just "too difficult," the fact Welsh has always subtly been styled as 'desirable' rather than 'essential' has led to a less-than-favourable outlook amidst the masses. And the 'second language' bug hasn't just infected those in English-medium education either. University was one of the first times I came across people my age who had received their education through Welsh. It was no secret to them that the vast majority of their former classmates mirrored a bigger picture across Wales' Welsh-medium education – that most parents of students attending Welsh-medium schools did not speak Welsh at home. To these young people, I was taken aback to hear that they also branded themselves as 'second language' – believing that one could only possess the 'mother tongue' tag if Welsh was also the language of the home. It's tough to argue considering, throughout their schooling, they would probably have regularly recognised students who spoke Welsh at home as having a greater Welsh vocabulary, more confidence when speaking, and a certain *je-ne-sais-quoi* when expressing themselves compared to those with little or no Welsh at home. Either way, the curse of 'second language' had struck again, with large numbers of Welsh-medium educated but no home Welsh students believing their ability in Welsh was second-rate to others. Subsequently there existed, and still exists today, an uncertainty among Wales' youth regarding the place of Welsh in their lives; many believing that Welsh belonged only to their education – regardless of their linguistic skills. This, ultimately, has led to a vast lack of confidence and desire to continue to use the language that, in truth, they could all no doubt speak to fantastic level.

But can there be a place for this increasingly unpopular term? Applying a 'second language' to one's learning has the potential to be an exciting prospect. Before becoming a reader for pleasure, books didn't appeal to me. I'd regularly get lost in complex story lines and would be put off from trying again for sometimes years. That was until I read a book shortly after I'd seen its film version. Knowing where the story was headed because of the film helped me through the book and still left a bit of room for more surprises where non-film content resided. This discovery made me question whether I could utilise my native language to support me through learning Welsh where putting myself into a mindset of a given topic via a 'comfortable' means might aid my language acquisition too. For example, reading a piece of text in English before then attempting to read it in Welsh sets the scene and context for the learner and helps to place previously unseen vocabulary. I recently bought the Welsh version of Tolkien's 'The Hobbit' but, even now as a fluent speaker with a degree in Welsh, I still know I'll trip up repeatedly until I read the English version first. I've come to peace with that – I just need to find time to read both now! This can be true of videos and music too where both English and Welsh versions exist. Later in this book I will reference a project led by myself along with other retro gaming enthusiasts which translated various '90s games into Welsh. The feedback from learners who were surprised at how much of the game they understood was almost certainly derived from remembering aspects of the game when they played it in English decades years ago. In all cases where English had already been used to 'set the scene' – be it in a book, a letter, a TV show or a super cool retro game – giving it a 'second try' in one's 'second [sic] language' offered huge scope to acquire new words and phrases, and reduced the need to pop back to a dictionary quite so much.

I've incorporated this idea into my teaching too; perhaps outlining a short story in English before tackling it in Welsh, or explaining the main idea of a letter in English prior to having students examine and answer questions on it later. As much as the old 'second language' as a teaching avenue has definitely run its course, the power of a learner's native language can't be ignored – even if these tactics are solely used *between* lessons when learning alone, reserving immersion tactics for classroom learning. As I'll explain later, we have English already… why not utilise it?

# TORRI'R MOWLD
*Breaking the mould*

Is a teacher allowed to challenge and offer passing thoughts for a drastic revolution in teaching their subject, or am I professionally obliged to blindly support the accepted provision whether I like it or not? Of course, I'm welcome to offer my own thoughts when the opportunity of an open forum arises, but those collaborations rarely go much further than the professionals in the room at the time. Consultation must be wholly public – so here are my two cents!

As far as is possible, make languages non-qualification based – perhaps just a teacher's comment listing each student's abilities in place of end-of-school certificates with a single letter to express the entire 16-year-long language journey. Big call, right? But for me, it's the jumping through hoops that prevents the 'relaxation' and patience necessary to acquire an additional language. In truth, I believe this model would work for most, if not all, arts-based subjects; removing the burden of bureaucracy and focussing wholly on ensuring real skills that can be both used in the wild and don't mean that students (wrongly) believe they gained nothing from their years of education in a subject. Fine, so this idea might need a tad more deliberation and planning than the few sentences I've offered here, but I truly believe it's something those in charge of education should consider.

With regards to younger high school students, I also have a cunning plan. Now, I reckon the average school affords around two hours per week to teaching languages which, over the course of around 39 weeks per academic year, equates to 78 hours of contact time. Over a three-year period from years 7 to 9, this ends up just shy of 240 hours. With me so far? Now, compare this to the work that Cyrsiau Trochi do in turning out nothing short of totally proficient speakers of Welsh. Cyrsiau Trochi are fast-track, full-immersion courses afforded to children of all ages who have little or no Welsh and will be moving to attend a Welsh-medium school. This covers young people moving from English-medium education in Wales to Welsh-medium, as well as children moving from all over the world to areas where only Welsh-medium schooling is available. Courses last for one term (usually September to December) before waving off their new Welsh speakers to their new Welsh-medium schools. Let's say that each course equates to four hours per day, five days per week for twelve weeks – 240 hours. Logistically it would present an initial nightmare for English-medium schools in Wales to implement, but is there a logic in spreading out the mind-blowing successes of Cyrsiau Trochi across a whole key stage in all schools in Wales? This is all before even starting on GCSE courses – something which will almost certainly yield far greater outcomes than we currently get. Perhaps a similar provision was the Education Department's aim all along, but it's clearly not a reality in, to my knowledge, any English-medium school in Wales. Granted, Cyrsiau Trochi are usually for younger students with sponges for brains in class sizes of around 10, but there must be a way of getting some of their achievements into mainstream English-medium schools'

Welsh lessons. I've yearned for years to pluck up the courage in my school to pitch this idea to the senior leadership team. I've imagined that, before rolling it out to everyone in every school, my pilot would initially identify students in year 6 (the final year of primary education in Wales) who possess strong Welsh skills and put them into a form group together. Then, instead of following the original scheme of work in Welsh lessons like everyone else in their year group, have them follow a different path akin to a Cwrs Trochi in their lessons. Keep a record of their progress over their initial 9 terms (3 years) in school and compare their eventual GCSE results to those who followed the original scheme. Even were this pilot to not produce fluent Welsh speakers, I can't see any occasion where this style of teaching would take them backwards – educationally or psychologically – in their dealing with the Welsh language. Unfortunately, my excitement and belief in this idea has not yet surpassed my apprehension of pitching it.

In reality, we're still some way off in ensuring the language is passed on to all young people via our current education provision. In this instance we should not, however, underestimate the fact that Welsh-medium education has been a huge part of the language surviving and flourishing in recent decades. From the first Welsh-medium primary school, Ysgol Gymraeg Aberystwyth, opened in 1939, to the present day where vast swatches of over-subscribed institutions are found across the country, Welsh-medium education is yielding far more Welsh speakers than produced via native-speakers passing the language on to their children could ever do. Today, all but one public school in Gwynedd provide their teaching through the medium of Welsh, offering the Cyrsiau Trochi to any children moving from English-medium to Welsh-medium schooling. Every other county in Wales has at least one Welsh-medium high school with ever-growing numbers of primary schools. It's an interesting fact that of all private schools in the British Isles, the only Welsh-medium one is in London.

As wonderful as these Welsh-medium provisions are, the further east we travel in Wales the less provisions there are. For example, out of nine secondary schools in the Wrexham area, only one, Ysgol Morgan Llwyd, is Welsh-medium. This poses a problem in that as more and more Welsh-medium primary schools open, more and more Welsh speaking young people will have to be turned away from continuing their studies into secondary education simply because of lack of spaces. In terms of percentages in this area, only 13% leave school having received their education through Welsh. According to StatsWales, the Welsh government's online repository for detailed statistical data for Wales, 16% of all Welsh pupils attend Welsh-medium schools with a further 10% attending schools considered bilingual, dual-medium, or English-medium but with significant Welsh provision. The current Parliament's aim [at the time of writing] is to increase these numbers to 30% by 2031 and to 40% by 2050.

It has been argued by academics and pressure groups alike that securing Welsh-medium education for all would ensure a bilingual populous. Where this is clearly true, the logistics and finances involved in realising this dream often throw a spanner in the works. The small number of 'bilingual schools' dotted around mostly consist of only one or two Welsh-medium 'streams' running alongside otherwise totally English-medium ones, rather than providing a mixture of some lessons through Welsh and some through English for *every* student. Parents often incorrectly state on documentation like census questionnaires that their child speaks Welsh because they attend a 'bilingual school' when, in reality, said students actually receive all their lessons through English. Students not attending the Welsh streams rarely possess any greater proficiency in the language when they eventually leave school than students attending schools where English is the only medium of education for all students. There may well, however, be potential in reforming bilingual schools to have all students learn at least some subjects through Welsh. As a result, even if only some subjects are subsequently available through Welsh with others through English, every student would still be able to converse in both tongues.

Similar logistical and financial challenges arise in implementing the idea of truly bilingual schooling are evident in a theory I believe has the potential to yield a totally bilingual population. Challenges of costs and training aside – I'm not an economist, after all – I believe that all primary schools in Wales should be Welsh-medium. I often meet students in the English-medium school where I work who've attended Welsh-medium primary schools and their Welsh is easily more than good enough to say they're fluent. They understand everything I say to them and the only 'mistakes' they make in using their language are no worse than the mistakes any English-speaking young person would make when using their English. These young people enjoy their Welsh lessons, enjoy the feeling when they're helping out other students in the class, and always come out with fantastic grades at GCSE Welsh (Second Language, granted). The biggest challenge in the theory lies in ensuring training for all the fantastic primary school teachers of Wales not fluent in Welsh. To go down the road of only employing teachers based on whether or not they were lucky enough to have received Welsh-medium education is a dangerous path to take and potentially denies Wales of some incredible and inspiring monoglot teachers, Welsh-born or otherwise. There's definitely weight in these ideas, but it will take nothing short of years of planning and adapting to realise them in practice. Howsoever Welsh-medium provision pans out in the future, and however long it takes to get to the promised land of a bilingual youth, it's calming to know that we seem to be slowly going in the right direction.

As a teacher outside of the Welsh-medium loop, it soon dawned on me that I had to come to peace with the fact producing fluent speakers via the 'second language' route is, at present, nothing more than a state afforded to perhaps one or two students (out of hundreds) every few years. I was one of the 'success stories' of the current system; I know of only two more from my year group of around 250 who've also ended up fluent in Welsh. For now, I've just had to accept that I must do what I can as a teacher. This is where my final philosophy came in. **Parch** – *Respect*. Perhaps students will never become fluent in God's own language by the time they leave school at 16, but I promise myself I'll do my utmost to ensure that they at least leave with a respect for the language. The odd **diolch** here and there. A promise to learn the anthem – not just the chorus. To stick up for and to talk up the language. To encourage others to give it a go rather than fall back onto the oh-so-common inevitability of just saying they didn't learn anything in their Welsh lessons. To send their own children to Welsh-medium schools. Something. Anything to prevent the language descending to less than even just an afterthought.

# DYSGWYR YN ADDYSGU
*Learners as teachers*

As a language teacher, being sympathetic towards students is something I believe to be really important. One doesn't even have to have necessarily gone through the process of acquiring a second or third language from scratch to understand the diverse needs of people who are going through it, but I reckon it helps.

For many students whose only interactions with Welsh come through me, I make it very clear to them that I learnt Welsh in much the same way as they are doing now. After putting their minds at ease that I am, in fact, still fully qualified to be imparting the language on them, I believe they respect the fact that we're all entitled to make mistakes and that fluency is most certainly not a binary outcome. I'm also proud to tell them that I'm still learning Welsh even after all these years of admitting fluency. I often speak of how, when listening to my wife speaking her flowing and natural Welsh, I'm jealous of how I still have to pause when I speak it myself to decide between using the formal or informal *'you.'*

During my second school placement whilst training towards my qualified teacher status, I was introduced to Phillip Lovell; at the time Head of the Welsh Department at Ysgol y Grango, Rhosllannerchrugog. Aside from his lively and interactive lessons – on which I base much of my teaching today – it was an email exchange that happened prior to my meeting him that has stayed with me. Upon discovering that he, like himself, had learnt Welsh, he hastened to add that we [non-native speakers] often make the best language teachers. This is by no means exclusive to those who've learnt the language out of choice, but displaying the same empathy we were shown as learners by our own teachers, coupled with the passion and enthusiasm that helped us to realise our own dream of becoming bilingual in the first place, is a strong mix for an educator to possess. I guess it's like building your own house as opposed to buying one – any homeowner loves and respects their home, but there's something different about being part of its construction from birth to life. Thinking back, at least two of the teachers who taught me in high school had learnt the language themselves too.

If you've never come across *Say Something in Welsh*, you're missing out. A Welsh learner himself, SSIW founder Aran Jones' technique of teaching via repetition and forcing one's brain to quickly create new synapses is nothing short of genius – even though he'll tell you himself that it's not exactly a new concept. But the way he applies it to language acquisition via scaffolding new words into pre-formed structures is, if you stick at it, highly effective. In his own words via his SSIW website, Aran shares the following about his course; *"I hoped that an mp3 course would be easier for people to stick with than a classroom course - I'd seen so many people drop out of those. I also hoped that what I thought I'd learned about language learning would help people start speaking Welsh faster than traditional courses. And I hoped that a free course would take away any excuse for people who moved to Welsh speaking communities not to learn the language. I hoped it would make a difference; that it would contribute something to the dream of building a real, genuine, successful future for this utterly precious language."*

After learning most of the Cornish and Manx that I now know from completing their respective courses on Aran's website, it'd have been nothing short of a huge missed opportunity to not think of as many ways as possible of horning his techniques into my own lessons. Over the years when introducing a new sentence structure, for example **hoffwn i** (*I would like to*) I'd have got my students to think of a couple of verbs to throw after it. Five or six lines in their books, read one each out afterwards, done. But no longer. Now I punt for repetition. Let the students choose a verb and keep getting the class as a whole* to repeat the sentence (ie **Hoffwn i** + verb) until we're ready for a new word to throw into the mix. Perhaps a different verb or perhaps a word to add onto what we've already done – each time popping back to the earlier words in between pelting them with brain-bruising, fast-paced questioning. Despite being teacher-led, I've found this to be far more effective than old fashioned drilling techniques (also teacher-led) as there's now a context rather than just a solitary list of words with little means to create a full sentence. It also gives the kids the ammunition to say things young people actually want to say in Welsh. It's like teaching a concept in maths parrot fashion versus teaching it with reference to real-life situations. There becomes a point, a reason, and a light at the end of the tunnel.

*I find getting the class as a whole to answer together to be a great 'subconscious' motivation builder. It offers a safety net to those unsure around the language. Of course, there are times when individuals must speak on their own, but I attempt to minimise this wherever I can – especially in earlier years. One student getting something wrong (even with their teacher admitting that he himself got more wrong than he did right when he was learning) in front of peers can lead to them hiding away for the remainder or the lesson and even forming the massively incorrect (yet, unfortunately understandable) view that they're just no good at languages. It happens and we must guard against it. Controlled shouting out of answers as a class will always bring the correct answer to the fore and drown out incorrect answers. To a young person who's easily embarrassed, this safety net often encourages far more interaction. And which kid doesn't love any excuse for shouting across a classroom?

# PWÊR A PHWYNT PWYNTIAU PŴER
*The power and point of PowerPoint*

When presented with any sort of technology, my mother's favourite phrase is *"What's wrong with old fashioned pen and paper?"* The answer, of course, is nothing, but the youth of today won't have any of it.

With this in mind, Welsh teachers have to be dynamic – sometimes more dynamic than teachers of any other subject. On top of being a subject that has been considered 'pointless' by so many for decades, the huge lack of materials and resources available for teenage learners hasn't helped the cause. The burden facing teachers to create their own stuff is far more daunting than the prospect of exploiting a potential gap in the market. Search any resource website for ideas on any subject and get inundated with flashy games, jazzy videos and even whole lesson plans complete with resources and homework tasks. Do the same for Welsh and you'll be lucky to find any worksheet that includes the name of a 'celebrity' or TV show any teenager these days has actually heard of.

Back when I was training in Llangollen, even then teachers were providing students with photocopies of hand-written worksheets they'd created to aid the current topic they were teaching. Few staff used visual aids on the boards and the only real opportunities students got away from their books was typing up the final draft of a 50-word pretend postcard from a place they'd never actually been. Thankfully, I can happily spend hours jazzing up worksheet and slideshows on a Sunday afternoon in front of the footy to hopefully ensure none of my students need to endure uninspiring resources. Thinking back even further to my own learning in school, one of the more exciting parts of any subject was when the old TV or OHP were rolled into the classroom. Everyone knew there was going to be a video or at least some sort of image on the board. Anything other than the teachers' scribbles was a blessing. These days, however, with media becoming more eye-catching and interactive all the time, no projected document or handwritten worksheet will satisfy today's young minds.

Nowadays it's thankfully not too uncommon for teachers to use interactive whiteboards and snazzy slideshows with embedded videos. I'm a huge fan of employing these modern marvels in my lessons because, for me personally, slideshows are essentially my lesson plans that remind me where I'm taking the learning next and, for the students, they are constant, colourful and dynamic visual aids. Another good thing about having a presentation for pretty much each lesson is that, if one part of the lesson didn't go as well as I expected or students struggled with a certain way I'd explained something, it was super easy to just edit the file ready for the next time it was used. Having prominent visuals also means that students whose concentration range is similar to that of a gnat are more likely to daydream looking at what's displayed on the board rather than watching the cow eating grass in the adjacent field. At the other end of the scale they offer an opportunity for keen students to work more independently. Independent working using visual stimuli also means students put their hands up less and subsequently don't feel as though they're struggling more than their peers and in need of my help.

It's been really interesting using these snazzy techniques with my adult classes too. They reckon I'm a right whiz-kid!

# CYMHELLIAD; AM GYTHRUDDO?
*Motivation; such an aggravation?*

Embarrassment can be the biggest killer of a love for *anything*, never mind a language. Surrounded by 29 other people of your age who, at lunch times your hormones are urging that you need to impress and look cool in front of, are now waiting for you as they sit and witness you struggle to pronounce a 6-letter Welsh word that everyone else can say perfectly. As a teacher, get this wrong and they're switched off for the lesson – and perhaps even forever. I guess it's mildly akin to parenting in that tickling your 10-year-old's sides at home gets giggles, but do it in front of their friends and don't expect to be spoken to for days.

Motivation is a huge deal for me. In times where some students rarely hear how well they're doing from other teachers or even from home, making Welsh the place they hear it can do wonders not just for our language, but for them as individuals. I've often targeted students harbouring a lack of motivation, got them to create a sentence in Welsh and praised them for it all lesson – often coming back to the same sentence (and back to heap praise on the student once again) multiple times. If there's going to be any parrot-fashion repetition in my classes, it'll be from me. Many times, the sentence I choose to 'over-praise' is one that I'm certain all other students in the class can also create. Subconsciously, the other students realise that they are more than capable of commanding the same praise also. Motivation complete.

My motivation techniques, however, are not just empty promises of wondrous outcomes. For example, I would never claim that a student is capable of achieving an A* grade if they weren't. The 'problem' is, and this is something I explain to my classes on a regular basis, they are all actually capable of achieving an A* grade. In the school in which I teach we use the popular setting system; one class which data tells us will likely achieve higher grades and another with less favourable data. However, in either class, I see the same knowledge and ability to create sentences. It's merely a lack of confidence (and often a lack of imagination) that holds back the 'lower ability' set and rarely their linguistic ability. Tell a musician that they possess some sort of divine talent with which they're simply born and they'll laugh at you. It's the same thing for students who believe that language acquisition is beyond them; it's just practise and self-belief.

In many instances, it tends to be subtlety that's the key to motivation. At times, when a student in the class asks for a word – especially one I'd expect most of the class to know, I pretend that I've genuinely forgotten it myself. I find the benefits of reminding students I'm still a learner too – even if I know full well what the word is – encourages others in the class to 'help me out.' Instead of singling someone out and damaging their confidence with a chorus of "*But I knew that word!*" "*So did I!*" "*Me too!*", showing them that I'm just as fallible as they are can be really effective.

From a psychological perspective, the art of teaching is the act of teaching. Ultimately it can be a tad annoying deep down when students giggle and inform you that you're the Welsh teacher and should therefore know every single word – especially when I actually do know the word for which they're asking. It does, however, all work out in the end when I get another opportunity to tell students that I learned Welsh via the same system they're experiencing and that their linguistic ability is way better than mine was at their age.

# AMDDIFFYN TAFODIAITH (RHAN 1)
*Defending dialect (Part 1)*

Hear about a burglary on the other side of the world and you wonder why someone's even bothering telling you. Hear about a burglary four streets away and you go out and buy new locks for your back door. It's a sad and unhealthy world view, but there's no doubting that our locality is intrinsically important to us.

In order to organise the teaching of Welsh (as a mother tongue or as a second language), standardisation of the language is required. In the case of Cornish which, up to the early 2000s, had four accepted spelling systems (owing to varying reconstructions throughout the 19th and 20th centuries) meant that it missed out on EU funding until around mid-2008 when those promoting the language finally agreed on a Standard Written Form. Having one standard language to learn makes obvious sense. However, as a strong believer in dialectal differences holding the keys to understanding the social histories and peculiarities of their localities, I tend to perceive the ironing out of local differences as an attack on the purity of the language – even if I do understand the need to have a 'common' and standardised version too.

I'll often teach words unique to our part of Wales (ie north east Wales in our case). Words like **ôd** (*snow*), **difie** (*Thursday*) and **snapin** (*snack, break*) instead of the standardised words (**eira**, **dydd Iau** and **byrbryd/egwyl** respectively) give students terms to 'defend.' Never mind learning language that's special to their home *nation*, I find arming them with terminology unique to their local towns and villages gives them even more of an incentive to defend, use and be proud of the language they know; all the while improving their overall skills. On top of this, we're also breathing life into terminology that, in many cases, is being lost at an alarming rate.

My wife is an incredible teacher and it's for two reasons I'm glad she's a primary school teacher; 1) because were she a secondary teacher like myself, it'd be far easier to compare us and she'd absolutely put me to shame every time and 2) because she teaches in Welsh-medium Ysgol Gymraeg Gwenffrwd in Treffynnon, I get to rob resources for her younger (but fluent Welsh) students and appropriate them for my own second-language learners.

I will, however, raise something I've raised many times with my wife. She usually tells me to piss off, but you guys don't get that pleasure. Being from Porthmadog, my wife speaks very different Welsh to me. Both are northern dialects so there aren't a huge number of differences but there are peculiar words and odd pronunciations we'll both use that are not commonplace in each other's dialect. It's an unfortunate yet all too common misconception that Welsh possess only two dialects. Either way, it's only natural for her to speak the language in which she's most comfortable. No one can bemoan that. But, and as I'll attempt to explain in 'Part 2' at the end of the book, how much could our schools be doing to help out our local dialects and giving learners a part of this language that's unique to them? Something for them to defend.

# PETHAU BYCHAIN
*Little things*

I've learnt that there are a multitude of effective and ineffective ways of correcting learners. Sometimes even 'forgetting' to correct ideas can be beneficial. We must, as teachers, ensure a balance between enough red pen (green in our school – less harsh) to encourage learners to keep working at their skills, but not too much to make them question why they even tried in the first place. As I've mentioned previously, each student is different, and the needs of every individual must be understood and addressed by their teachers – not such a revolutionary idea, but a solid one. It represents one of the biggest challenges of teaching but, when you know you've got it right, the examination results and just general positivity towards Welsh is amazing.

Depending on the ability of the individual I'm teaching, I've begun dropping mutations that might cloud the meaning of the word it effects. In the eyes of some this is laziness and merely teaches bad habits, but tell me, as a fluent speaker, that you can't understand this statement; **mae gen' i *cath***. Other times I won't speak in full Welsh sentences – dropping a few English words into what I say. It's not to appear 'cool' or even simply to ensure understanding. Most of the time I do it to keep learners on their toes and have them experience the phenomenon of linguistic code-switching. For students who require a little more time to process language, it can also afford them a breather to ensure they're not left behind.

In response to a tweet I posted asking Welsh speakers to 'own up' to which English words they used when speaking Welsh and *vice versa*, Dr Bethan Tovey-Walsh responded that she was following the thread with great interest as this very notion was to be part of her PhD research into code-switching and the inclusion of 'discourse markers' (like '***jyst***' and '***so***') that have embedded themselves into modern Welsh speech. Bethan argues against code-switching being perceived as 'laziness' and defends her belief that it represents *"normal behaviour, especially when your audience understands both languages."* Interestingly she went on to say in her tweet to me that *"It's how our brains work. Some [...] do it more, some less. You can suppress it, but that takes energy and effort, so it makes you less efficient."* Bethan later offered that both standardised and 'slang' Welsh should be taught to students learning Welsh but also agreed with me that time constraints hindering teachers means that doing this in practice is nigh on impossible. We both shared my belief that Welsh teachers and tutors could favour '**bratiaith**' (a term used by Welsh speakers to describe common, less formal language) to get learners' Welsh to a standard they're more likely to hear in the wild, as well the fact the door would then be left open to any student wishing to pursue more formal language with an already sound basis in it. As teachers we must weigh up what's important; getting a handful of students to possess perfect Welsh or getting most students to have Welsh that's good enough for the streets on which the language lives. For better or worse, my philosophy favours the latter.

Another ploy of mine – similar to the code-switching idea – is when I'm explaining something in Welsh I'll pause to throw in English translations for words I deem potentially difficult or simply new and then go back to the start of the sentence to say it all again without the translation. For example, I might say something like this: "**Heddiw rydyn ni'n mynd i ddarllen disgrifiad** *description* **disgrifiad. Rydyn ni'n mynd i ddarllen disgrifiad o berson.**" – *Today we're going to read a description of a person*. Going back once I'd translated a particular word (or words) not only normalises it for the next time they hear it (in these cases just a few seconds later), but it also instils a subtle confidence in the students that they're only a few words off total comprehension of much of what I say. It takes a little longer than merely saying it all in English, but any excuse to be repeating instructions to teenagers is always a winner anyway!

Finally, and this one's a real bugbear of mine. As teachers we all love it when students use 'incidental' Welsh without prompting, and ensuring they know stuff like asking to go to the loo and how to ask to borrow a pen gives us a little lump in our throats knowing we've forged the situation where a young person felt confident and comfortable enough to use their Welsh with us. But no matter what, do not let them say '*Beth ydy [word/phrase] yn Gymraeg?*' Have them say something like '*Beth ydy'r gair am [word/phrase]?*' You may think I'm pedantic here but asking what a word is *in Welsh* immediately creates a subtle reminder that Welsh is their *other language* when it should be an additional one. Coaxing young people away from being aware of the target language, even via means a subtle as this, really helps in the quest to normalise Welsh.

# IAITH LAW
## *Hand signals*

Continuing with subtleties; hand signals are super effective – and I don't mean the ones that immediately came to your head when you first read that! For example, when I talk about **darllen paragraff** (*reading a paragraph*), I will open my hands to feign opening a book. Students are usually quite fine with the word **paragraff**! I will also open and close one hand like an opening and closing mouth when I say **siarad**, point to my eyes when I say **gweld**, and pretend to be holding binoculars when I say **gwylio**.

The removal of English encourages reliance on the target language, and it doesn't just work with simple vocabulary either. One part of Welsh that can confuse Welsh learners (even if most of the world's languages outside of English function in this way) is placing adjectives *after* nouns rather than before. A simple gesture of swapping my hands over one another immediately shows or reminds students that a ***pinc car*** should be a **car pinc**. Once you've explained the concept and coupled it with the visual act of swapping hands, soon enough only the signal is sufficient to remind the students. When I initially explain how most adjectives follow nouns in Welsh, I often tell the morbid tale (that I fabricated myself) of two treasure hunters on their death beds – one English speaking and the other Welsh speaking. Sensing their ends, they decide to tell their gathered families the whereabouts of their buried gold. The English speaker begins with his description of the area around his treasure. With a sputtering cough signifying his terminal breaths, s/he explains that the treasure is under the *"old, flimsy, grey…."* and death takes them away. The Welsh speaker's family hear first that the treasure was buried under the garden shed all along. The need to describe it afterwards is trivial. Okay, so it's hardly the greatest story ever told but it seems to get the point across to the students successfully.

Modern Welsh is lazy in comparison to its literary sibling. The tendency for native speakers to say stuff like '**cwcio**' instead of '**coginio**' and '**dreifio**' instead of '**gyrru**' can often be too easy to avoid. It's a huge bug with many purists who do their best to totally avoid any code-switching. For learners, however, these *Wenglish* words offer them free vocabulary that's ready to go from the off…. so long as they put a bit of a Welsh accent on it when they say it, right? Perhaps I'll teach words like '**gwersylla**' to younger students when we talk about types of holidays, but if a year 11 student only a week away from starting a multitude of examinations for around 10 different subjects after a rigorous few months of cramming revision into their brains asks me how to say '*camping*' in Welsh, you can bet their minds will be far more grateful of hearing me say '**campio**.' Perhaps this is another argument against the current system of standardised testing for Welsh as a school subject, but as it stands, at least '**campio**' is a word they'll commonly hear in Welsh and, more importantly, is one that will be understood by any fluent speaker who hears or reads it.

It can, of course, be tough getting learners of any age whose brains are ready for Welsh, to actually recognise a token English addition to a sentence but the fact is they're common place in modern speech. Psychologically, it provides learners with a safety net as they make the leap from using the language in just the classroom to out in the wild.

In similar fashion when listening to learners speak, 'correcting' them for pronouncing *'pizza'* in an 'English' way rather than the *Welshier* '**pitsa**' is an abomination. This leads to another pet hate of mine where some teachers spend hours picking on students not trilling (or rolling) their 'R' sounds. This can be a trait of French teachers too whose native language also incorporates said sound. Teachers in the north east can get away with letting students off for this because trilling Rs is sparingly done around here – even among many native speakers. But no matter where you teach, picking up on things like these is a total waste of time. Get your priorities right and get over it, otherwise your learners will be making their own hand signals at you behind your back.

# TRAPIAU
*Traps*

When you get a class of hungry-to-learn sponges, it can be all too common for them to believe their Welsh has to be as good as their English straight away. While I'll never be someone who disrespects ambition, it's important for young people to know two things. The first is that learning a language is a journey and keeping things simple now and again in order to build on them later is an integral part of the process. It's not that we're 'slowing them down' at all, it's that we're ensuring we strengthen what they have before we shoot off onto something else. As I always say, even simple words for colours and numbers are just as useful at GCSE and A Level as are the intricate phrases offering opinions on detailed subjects.

The second point is that Welsh, in comparison to English, is a rather 'simplistic' language. This obviously doesn't mean that anything written or said in English cannot be expressed in Welsh, but it's often the case that finding a 'simpler,' more 'manageable' way to express one's English sentence before working towards expressing it in Welsh still yields a perfectly acceptable (and often better) expression in Welsh. For example, I'll often encourage students who want to say something like "*My village possesses ample facilities for younger residents*" (yep, some do ask me to help with sentences like that!) to think of a simpler way to express it. A discussion evolves in which we agree that something like "*There are a lot of facilities for young people here*" is easier to work with while still expressing the same idea. The subsequent translation, "**Mae lot o gyfleusterau i bobl ifanc yma**" is a far more accessible way of expressing the sentence – rather than trying to explain a whole host of new terminology and mutations in a straight translation of their initial idea; "**Mae gan fy mhentref ddigon o gyfleusterau i drigolion iau.**" At the very least, encouraging students to think of 'other' ways to express their English is a fantastic yet subtle way of nurturing their problem-solving skills too.

Another similar trap into which students of all ages fall is the way that some Welsh constructions 'make no sense' in English. It's a different language after all and, in these cases, teachers must use caution to explain this fact. A post on a Welsh Learners Facebook group where someone was struggling with the Welsh construction for '*I must*' reminded me of this common confusion amongst younger learners. In this Facebook case, the learner wondered why the Welsh equivalent was '**mae'n rhaid i fi**' and he pondered how to get his head around it. I explained the concept to him just as I explain it to my students. Literally, '**mae'n rhaid i fi**' translates as '*it is necessary for me to...*' which, on initial viewing, looks rather silly – even if it does make sense fundamentally. When teaching concepts like this, I will always explain the literal translation first to ensure students see that there's method in the madness and that Welsh isn't out to trip you up... on purpose, anyway! With some classes, I often stop using the *correct* English format completely, preferring to ask students to translate '*it's necessary for me to go*' rather than '*I have to go.*'

Traps aren't just things into which students fall. Teachers can, and often do, slip up too. With it being so easy to simply head straight for Google Translate, students these days rarely expose themselves to something that is indescribably efficient in the process of learning a language – just giving it a go. In school time and especially during examinations, this online resource is not available to students and so they're forced to forge what they want to express on their own. It can be just as easy for a teacher to fall into the trap of just blindly translating swathes of sentences for students as it can be for them to chuck everything through online translators. *"Miss/Sir, beth ydy [huge sentence] yn Gymraeg?"* "Oh, I'll just write it on the board for you!" One of my favourite things to do these days is to encourage them to try it first. Not only does it force learners to break and re-form linguistic synapses in their brains, but it also gives the teacher a bit of breathing space in what can quickly turn into thirty hands up all at once asking for 30-word sentences each. There's nothing wrong with offering help and phrases to students, but it's once again down to us as teachers to identify occasions when we need to help, and when we can let them get on with it themselves. Tough love and all that.

# DWEUD BETH SY' GEN' TI
*Say what you've got*

Back when school budgets were twice the size they are now, I remember attending a conference weekend down in Cardiff. The whole weekend was a great chance to not only hear seminars led by successful teachers and educators, but also a great opportunity to socialise with other teachers where conversation always ended up with sharing ideas that worked for them. One such speaker that weekend was Jo Knell. Author of libraries of dynamic textbooks and swathes of resources, her knowledge in the field of teaching Welsh in English-medium schools was, and probably still is, second to none. On top of the insane amount of tactics and techniques she shared in those few hours, it was her determination to not worry too much about reading and writing Welsh that stayed with me. In no way did she discourage and underestimate the power of reading and writing but, for students in English-medium schools at least, having the ability to *speak* a language meant that the ability to read and write it tended to naturally follow without a great deal of work. It's why weightings for levelling and grading students is always at least 50% speaking work at all levels of the curriculum. The only problem is that once students hit their early teens, getting them to talk in their native language can be a chore – never mind doing it in their second or third language and in front of their peers.

Knell was right, of course. The number of 50+ year-olds I know who speak Welsh fluently but struggle writing it is incredible.

The likelihood that this generation were denied Welsh education – sometimes because no Welsh-medium schools were available and sometimes because parents chose to put them through English-medium education but spoke Welsh at home.

How many times have you come across someone on social media whose posts and comments are littered with grammatical and spelling errors? Now before you label me as a member of the Language Police, I only go after someone's poor spelling and grammar if they're arguing with me on Twitter trying to tell me that Welsh is pointless. My point here is that, had the same conversation been had face-to-face, then mixing up spellings like *'your'* and *'you're'* go unnoticed. It's often described as the most difficult part of learning any acquisition – especially when it's teenagers you're trying to get to speak – but speaking offers us all a safety net that just isn't there to catch us when we write.

Of course, reading and writing are important and should never be actively discouraged, but if, for the time being at least, it's a greater number of *speakers* we're yearning for....

After all, the goal at the end of language learning is to be able to say '**Dw i'n gallu *siarad* Cymraeg**,' not '**Dw i'n gallu *darllen* Cymraeg**,' right?

# ATAL Y TRAI
## *Preventing the ebb*

Teaching Welsh to high-school students was never going to be enough for me. If I could make youngsters find a point in Welsh, why couldn't I do it elsewhere? Over the past few years, I've put on free Welsh sessions in my local area and shoved up posters in bus stops with translations of phrases like 'this bus stop smells' and 'three came along at once' with the sole aim of bringing Welsh to those who simply aren't exposed to the language other than on the bottom halves of road signage. I attend a fortnightly informal conversation group where fluent speakers come to chat about, well, anything, and people with little or no Welsh come to try out what they can or even to simply listen and not speak at all. Ooo, and I've straight up refused to ever say the words *'thank you'* ever again – everyone in Wales knows what diolch means, right?

As I mentioned at the beginning of this book, I grew up close to the border with Cheshire – not exactly a Welsh-speaking stronghold these days – and my first teaching job took me to a place where, when I looked out of my eastern windows, I could see the sign welcoming people to Shropshire. *"Why are we learning Welsh? I'm English"* was a common thing to hear from the older students when I first started. I know that most were just attempting to show the new teacher stood before them that they'd been in the school longer than he had rather than actually bemoaning learning Welsh, but there were some who genuinely believed that being born in England meant that they should be exempt from this huge part of Wales' devolved education system. It's like attending school in Sweden and bemoaning having to learn Swedish. Despite not hearing such questions at all in recent years, I know full well this moaning still happens in some places.

Essentially, it's a fundamental problem. The most effective way to predict a bad attitude towards a language amongst young people is sadly yet commonly a bad attitude from their parents. You ask most adults these days about their view on Welsh and they'll tell you they'd love to speak the language, but their "teacher put them off back in school"; stating how their lessons were boring and uninspiring. Perhaps that's truly the case, but it can often be down to an intrinsic poor attitude from themselves that ultimately leads to the detriment of their children – the 'uninspiring lessons' being merely their scapegoat. It's tougher again to tackle the views of English-born parents who've moved to Wales only to find their children learning a language they genuinely thought was just an elaborate joke.

Up until the World Wars, languages other than English were not only discouraged in the British Isles, they were trodden into the dirt. On a visit some years ago to *Thie Tashtee Vannin* (The Manx National Museum) in Douglas, there was a small exhibit dedicated to the Manx language. One section recalled people's memories of the language once considered extinct by UNESCO – despite the island boasting a Manx-medium primary school (*Bunscoll Ghaelgagh*) in the village of Saint John's since 2001. One such memory by Ramsey-resident, Henry Quayle, read;

*"My father and mother could all talk Manx, though they weren't encouraging the children to speak it. The parents would be wanting the children to speak English and not Manx. They would not be wanting them to appear backward compared with others."* Sound familiar, perhaps? The act of turning the hearts and minds of people whose families over centuries only dealt in Manx (and other minority languages) is quite the feat, it must be said.

Children inevitably soak up the prejudices of their parents and those around them – a trend that will forever continue until a whole generation and society decides enough is enough. If you and I can do something to fight this trend, we'll have done well. We may not be teaching the next generation to be *fluent* in Welsh, but leaving them with a positive attitude towards the language might just encourage more and more young people to take up the language in the future; perhaps encourage their own children to make the most of Welsh lessons in school, or even make them think seriously about sending their little ones to a Welsh-medium school. Considering it's taken around 800 years to batter our language into its current state, I'll rest happy knowing that we were the ones who broke the plummeting trend.

The Welsh language from southern Scotland downwards lost the Welsh language (or archaic forms of it) one word at a time until only anglicised place-names – masking their true Welsh origin – remained. But this erosion can be reversed. There are nations on the other side of the planet whose languages have been completely displaced by English so to consider that Wales shares a land border (longer than those of Cornwall and Scotland) with a nation whose language has become the global tongue of choice and still survived speaks volumes for the passion and determination of the Welsh towards their linguistic heritage.

With a little encouragement, we can all be inspired to do our bit to help. Previously saddened by a lack of Welsh literature and signage throughout restaurants and local businesses', nowadays I prefer to offer them my services to translate anything free of charge. We have to ensure there's a place for Welsh in people's lives – even if it's something as small as one phrase per generation. Throwing a Welsh phrase into your own daily life is like throwing chocolate chips into a Welsh cake (sacrilege to some but I reckon they're beautiful!) or a dash of whisk(e)y in your tea. It spices everything up. Teaching can most definitely offer the means to go on in Welsh, but it certainly doesn't answer *all* the questions.

# YR HEN A ŴYR
*The older folks know best*

Finally, it was an untapped passion to extend my teaching outside of the school environment that became an itch I constantly yearned to scratch. In mid-2019 I applied to teach Welsh to adults at an evening class run by **Dysgu Cymraeg Gogledd Ddwyrain** and **Coleg Cambria**, the north east's further education college. By September I was realising another personal dream and stood before a class of 10 paying students who, for a whole multitude of reasons, wanted to learn Welsh. Some were there just to better themselves. Some were primary school teachers and wanted to utilise more Welsh in their classes. Others wanted to reconnect with a language that was lost somewhere in the family tree. Some worked for companies who visited both English and Welsh-medium schools on pastoral days. Some just liked an excuse to get out of the house.

After a rigorous briefing on how lecturing Welsh as a college tutor differed from teaching it in schools – massively, by the way – the final piece of advice my new colleague gave me was "**jyst siaradwch Gymraeg efo nhw!**" – *just speak Welsh with them!* For better or worse, this was not something for which I'd ever got used to doing in my previous decade teaching in a secondary school (aside from with my sixth form groups) and, considering my new adult class were only in their second year of the entire course, this was not something for which I was at all prepared to hear two minutes before I was due to introduce myself and to begin teaching them. Of course, I knew I could speak Welsh and that my lesson was ready, but actually being conscious to not speak English to ten people who, in my mind, surely couldn't have had *that* good a grasp on Welsh scared the hell out of me. But guess what? It bloody worked. Of course, I had to explain the odd concept in English and translate a few things for them but speaking mostly Welsh to students was a new and amazing feeling. In short, if you're an adult looking to take up the challenge of learning Welsh, wonderful apps and online games aside, being in a classroom environment really can't be beaten. Sign up!

# GWRW CYMRAEG
*Welsh guru*

When one reads books offering tips to teachers about how to get students more interested in languages etc, one can often be left in awe at the authors' talents. It's the same with watching football – we go to enjoy the game and watch how players act and react in different situations but forever know we'll never be as good a footballer as the players on display. Well, I do anyway. Sometimes, we can become so disillusioned and become put off before taking the time to believe in ourselves. When I wake up on the first morning of our annual lads' camping trip with hair sticking up in all directions, sleepy eyes and the torso part of my rolled-up grey hoody sweatily stuck to the side of my face because I forgot my pillow, I'm in no rush to take a selfie for my Facebook profile. Why? Because 99% of us only show our best sides on social media. It's easy to presume that someone posting one photograph in three weeks of a sunset across a north Wales beach is living the dream, when the other twenty days they're working in a job they no longer enjoy moaning at the unrelenting rain.

The tactics and tips I've included in this book are like the sunset photographs I whack on Instagram. They're things I found to work and have enjoyed but – and it's a big but – if you think this stuff works all day every day then you'll be sorely mistaken. Getting students to love a language is hard – especially in a world that's using English (a language our students already speak) so frequently and so prominently. In the case of teaching

Welsh, we can't even bring in some super-cool French or German person to explain to our kids how super-cool France or Germany is because as Welsh speakers, the said super-cool person probably already lives in Wales like the rest of us. Hardly exotic! If your next thought is bringing a Patagonian over, let me know which magic money tree you're using and I'll get the invitations out. The Welsh speakers that students come across are the ones they already know from local Welsh-medium schools and in their communities. We are all already Welsh. What we could (or should) encourage is getting our already-fluent populous to use their Welsh *first*!

I'm not some language-teaching guru – far from it. I make mistakes and I have bad lessons, bad days, and even bad weeks just like everyone else. These are merely ideas I wanted to share with you. If you're a teacher, get your morals and philosophies correct. Ensure all children leave your lessons with a few more words and phrases than before they walked in and, perhaps more importantly, do your level best to ensure they leave with a passion, a respect, and a love for the language. These are three things that rub off rather well if you can parade them well enough. Finally, always remember that we're not *forcing* the language on students; we're bringing their Welsh out of them as an amalgamation and a continuation of the years of Welsh to which they've been exposed since they started school. Whether you're a teacher in any capacity or not, I hope you've taken something from this chapter.

# PENNOD 3
# DYSGU'R IAITH – Learning the Language

## NI ALLWCH FETHU
*You can't fail*

It is said (although also widely contested to be untrue) that, upon inventing the light bulb, Thomas Edison admitted to multiple prior failings before he eventually succeeded. Now often spotted as a framed motivational fact in workplaces across the globe, Edison is said to have taken pride in the thousands of 'failed' attempts at achieving his aim. On top of inventing the light bulb, Edison realised thousands of ways to *not* make a light bulb – all of which as important as each other, and ultimately, as important as the invention itself in the grand scheme of his quest.

In this chapter (and throughout this book) I offer paths to fluency that have either worked for me or that have worked for others around me. With a bit of luck, some will be of use in your own personal quest and some will simply be ways that, via attempting them in practice, will merely turn out to be means by which you *didn't* find success. Of course, failing once is in no way an excuse to never try a method again, but in any case, the little Welsh you inevitably learn via an ineffective method is still *some* Welsh and nothing will be a waste. The aim of this chapter is to arm you with new ideas that work for you; untrodden paths to wherever you desire your Welsh language journey to go.

Teaching Welsh meant I needed to learn *how* people learned – every single way! Every single path and avenue for learning; be they of learning a language or simply of learning in general. Being on your toes as a learner or a teacher is to be on the cutting edge of change; to adapt to the many situations, challenges, and eventualities one might face. The most important thing I've learned since becoming a teacher is that learners must be exposed to as many different ways of learning as possible. As frustrating and 'un-logistical' as it can sometimes be, there's absolutely no denying that it's the learners themselves who must decide and appropriate the ways that work for them as they find their way to competency in a subject. This is the same for learners of any age; it has to begin with themselves.

# CAMAU CYNTAF
*First steps*

Before embarking on bridging the gaps between one's linguistic aspirations and the ability to apply them in real-life situations, one must start where all journeys start; at the beginning. When I'm asked by prospective learners where to begin with acquiring Welsh in their own time, my answer to them is clear… one must have a reason.

That reason can be for family – perhaps a child attends a Welsh-medium school. It can be because one has moved to Wales and wishes to integrate themselves with the language around them. Perhaps one's job deals regularly (or even irregularly) with people whose preferred means of communication is Welsh. It can be for those who simply enjoy the challenge of learning another language – whether they will ever find a practical use for it or not. My reason was because I am Welsh; because learning the language of those who forged the nation where I first saw daylight offered me a connection to a people I knew I'd never know, but to whom I felt an intrinsic debt.

There are innumerable and infinite possible reasons to be had. My advice is not to waste time trying to conjure yours up from thin air, but to discover it. There is always a reason whether you're currently aware of it or not. It's there; and the Welsh language is grateful to you for it.

# MYND 'NÔL AR Y CEFFYL
*Getting back on the horse*

It's no secret that most of the people who decide to take up learning Welsh are Welsh themselves. They live in Wales, were brought up here and received their education here. Recommencing learning Welsh as an adult can be daunting – especially when you feel pressured that you've already had at least some education as a child. In this case, it's common to want to pretend you have zero Welsh; believing your ability should currently be far greater than you believe it to be. Considering all the years one spends learning Welsh over some 15 years at school, many feel embarrassed and, more worryingly, some wrongly concede that they must simply be unable to learn Welsh. If it didn't happen after all those years of education as a child, what are the chances of picking it up later in life, right?

Attempts to avoid cliché in this instance are impossible; it really is just like riding a bike. My stag do was over in Hamburg in 2018 and, just in case the lads chucked me into some, shall we say, awkward situations, I decided to prepare myself by cram-learning German on Duolingo. It had been some 14 years since I'd last seriously looked at the language as a fresh-faced GCSE student so my concerns that I'd be able to express anything other than *'Zwei Bier, bitte,'* (*Two beers, please*) were highly worrying. Incidentally, that was *not* the phrase I'd need after being force-fed ale by the lads since the early hours. My Duolingo German journey began as just a huge frustration. If I had a Euro for each time I uttered the words *'Aww, I know this one!'* immediately followed by, *'Damn, I did know that one!'* I'd have had enough cash to bribe the German bar staff to feed me non-alcoholic pints on the sly. Even so, I stuck with it and the words stuck in my head far quicker than I first imagined. I completed the course with a few weeks to spare before our weekend away and, without going into detail about *how*, my German proficiency got me out of a couple of interesting situations... or at least softened their intended blows!

Welsh will be no different for you. Many people who tell me they're going to try Welsh on Duolingo inform me that they can't believe how quickly they race through the initial stages. Of course, the learning gets more difficult and getting stuck multiple times on one particular sentence (often a totally useless one like *'Owen has no parsnips'*) can be gut-wrenching, but perseverance always pays off. Evening classes are no different – in fact, they can often be even nicer on former school learners when one considers that some members of the evening class begin having had literally *zero* prior schooling of Welsh. The point is to believe in yourself and certainly not blame yourself for an education system that, for all it's good features, rarely produces proficient speakers. It's not the fault of the system, it's just that, in its current guise, learning needs to continue after leaving school. You wouldn't want to hear your doctor inform you that their only knowledge of biology and chemistry is what they learned at A-level, would you? It's no different for a *re-learner* and, even though our lives may have taken us away from continuing our Welsh knowledge after school, we lose what we'd learnt at a surprisingly slow rate. Something that is reversed far quicker than many imagine.

## DW I'N BAROD
*I'm ready*

We live in a time where languages can never die. Even languages described as 'extinct' are stored in multitudes of books, journals, publications, and, of course, the world wide web; many complete with grammar notes, verb tables and lexicons galore. Name a language and, with a bit of thought and patience, you will discover at least something to learn. Thankfully, Welsh remains a thriving and living language which means the opportunities to throw oneself into it exist readily – if one knows where to look. For those wishing to tread a path requiring less 'bravery' but with a subsequently high potential for linguistic embarrassment, there is no limit to the resources available to obtain at least a decent 'footing' in Welsh before letting loose in conversations.

Despite not being at all *essential* to learning Welsh, willingness to part with hard-earned cash can certainly help you on your way. It's rare to find Welsh classes that are free (unless you can convince a Welsh-speaking mate to put on a few – I did mine for a local charity) but it's not rare to find groups at reasonable prices. Whether sitting in a classroom in school was your cup of tea or not, on a personal note I can't deny how effective being in a learning mindset along with others sharing your own curiosities and apprehensions led by an inspiring teacher is. I've witnessed it for myself. I've decided to learn languages on my own accord, purchased books and downloaded apps only to bite the bullet, sign up for a class or go to a meet-up and find I'd learn twice as much in one session as I had done in weeks of moping around flicking pages and taping pairs of words on my phone. I once invited Irish learners from the north east (and much of the north west of England too) to meet up for an hour to speak Irish in my local pub. I wasn't at all nervous in posting the event because, honestly, I didn't think anyone would show up. I went to the pub knowing that, when no one inevitably turned up, I could at least sink a cold pint of Wrexham Lager and go a couple more lessons on Duolingo before bed. I managed to get my pint, but I drank it in the company of three ladies who were learning Irish in the Liverpool area. With no chance of making a nervous dash for it, I threw myself in and ended up loving it. I was understanding so much and was actually speaking Irish myself. I won't forget that day in a hurry and I'm aching to do it again in the future.

If you can, sign up to a class. Seriously, just do it. Do not think for one second that you won't get anything out of it – that's impossible. And when you turn up for your first class or your first social meet-up, humbly remember that there'll always be people there who've been exposed to more Welsh than you and will, therefore, make you feel like you're behind before you've even started... even though you're not. In the same way, there will always be people there who don't pick up words and grammar and syntax as quickly as you. Before you bemoan those who seem to just become human sponges and soak up seemingly everything, remember that, to at least one other person in that room, you too are a human sponge.

Put simply, joining a class is a fantastic thing to do, but ensure you go with an open mind and a knowledge that, no matter how you learn, there are good days and bad days. Don't be quick to judge your new class by the first lesson either. Stick at it and give your all – welcome feeling physically drained after each one. Just like learners, us teachers we have bad lessons, bad days, and even bad weeks too. We often try things and they don't work – it's how we improve our own practice. Knowing this, learners shouldn't jump to conclusions that they're new tutor isn't for them and one bad experience or a difficult task should never alone be how a tutor is judged. I remember one of my college students email me privately after a lesson saying I often rushed over things without making sure they were completely clear first. The first thing I did was take a screenshot of the message and pasted it at the start of every single one of my PowerPoint slideshows to remind me to slow down, ensure understanding before moving on, and always pause for questions. You'll be hard pressed to find another tutor who wouldn't do something similar, I assure you.

As I hope I've made clear throughout this chapter and this whole book, we're all different and we all experience things in different ways. What works for one never – and I truly mean never – works for every single other learner. And, if you're one who's currently putting off learning Welsh at night class because you think you're "too old to learn Welsh," I present you with a fantastic tweet from @Penbrynhir (Dr Jen Llywelyn) I received when discussing how to encourage newbies to take up Welsh: *"It's not their brain that's too old, it's their attitude."*

You might not know it yet but you're ready. The road isn't an easy one, but those occasions where you get to finally let loose your skills in the wild makes it all worthwhile. Whichsoever road you take, be willing to accept this life-changing journey as one that's for the sake of something for which you'll probably never receive financial royalties. Whatever your reason behind running your marathon, run it with others. And remember, this one's not a race.

# AR Y FFORDD YN BAROD
*Already on the way*

Earlier in the book, I mentioned how code-switching, as well as the odd inclusion of words like *'obviously'* and *'really'* etc, have found their way into common Welsh speak.

The tendency for learners is to avoid this steadfastly – something historically done around 150 years ago among east Wales-dwelling speakers of Welsh. When completing my university dissertation on the state of the language in north east Wales, I learned that many residents at the time would prefer long pauses in conversations to remember the correct Welsh term for something, rather than quickly throwing in an English word for ease. The difference between speakers from then and now is that those in the 18th century did their level best to avoid dropping in English words almost as an act of defiance in a rapidly changing linguistic situation, whereas learners these days tend to do their best to avoid English to largely prevent being accused of possessing less-than-adequate skills in the language.

The point is that, these days, chucking in English words is commonplace and is hugely accepted (and utilised) by the native-speaking masses. The whole concept, on the face of it, might seem rather positive for learners who don't yet possess the Welsh for every single word. However, I've found that tuning one's mind as a learner into not only trying to comprehend the Welsh they're hearing, but also tuning into the off chance they might hear English words seamlessly thrown into random sentences at random times can often throw us off. *"Did they just say an English word there? Wait, now I've missed the rest of what they were saying!"*

My advice here is unfortunately not a quick-fix. There are no words of wisdom to help learners tackle these common situations other than to be ready for it; something difficult to acquire without throwing oneself into the deep end and using it. Furthermore, when speaking Welsh yourself, embrace the fact that no one will bemoan your using of the odd English word in what you say. In fact, I still often shove whole sentences of English within otherwise totally Welsh interactions and no one bats an eyelid.

As I said, there are positive cases to be taken from all this. Aside from knowing you'll never be judged poorly for using English in what you say, there are huge swathes of 'real' Welsh words that are actually insanely similar (and even sometimes exactly the same) as their English equivalents. When considering words like **coffi** (*coffee*), **golff** (*golf*), **gitâr** (*guitar*), **siarc** (*shark*), **trên** (*train*), **caffi** (*café*), **desg** (*desk*), **siaced** (*jacket*), **roced** (*rocket*), rygbi (*rugby*), **Mecsico** (*Mexico*), **wal** (*wall*), **car** (*car*), **siocled** (*chocolate*) etc, learners would do worse than to realise they already possess loads of Welsh vocabulary without having to actually sit down and learn new words from scratch. In truth, there's a decent chance that a learner awkwardly believing they're relying on an English word when speaking Welsh might unknowingly be yielding the accepted Welsh term anyway.

The common response by 'opponents' to the Welsh language is that we just rob words from English because our Welsh language is too old or too silly to possess its own terminology. The fact is that most of the words that, to the untrained eye, might seem just like a *Welshified* version of an English word – such as *ambulance* > **ambiwlans** for example – are actually borrowed from the original language from whence both derived anyway; in the case of **ambiwlans**, *'ambulat-'* in Latin means *'walking'* – a nod to the fact that ambulances are, in essence, *'walking'* or mobile hospitals.

Don't think this is at all a one way street and that English didn't appropriate any words from our Celtic languages either. *Bard* (< **bardd**), *car* (< **cerbyd**), *flannel* (< **gwlanen**) and *kist* (< **cist**) – among many others – all derive from words us Welsh had already been using for centuries prior. *Slogan* (from Gaelic **'sluagh gairm'** meaning *'battle cry'*), *whisk(e)y* (from Gaelic and Irish **'uisge/uisce beatha'** meaning *'the water of life'*), *smashing* (from Irish **'is maith (é) sin'** means *'that's good'*), and the parting phrase *so long* (from Irish **'slán'** meaning *'goodbye'*) represent just some of the words borrowed from our Gaelic cousins too. In the case of *'whisk(e)y,'* a common joke amongst Gaels is that, because the English word only derives from the part of the Gaelic term that means *'water,'* only true Celts can handle the real stuff.

Chin chin... which is vulgar Chinese for *'cheers'*... and Japanese for *'penis.'*

# ADNODDAU
## *Resources*

An inability to attend evening courses doesn't at all mean that there's no place for extra, non-classroom-based aid. Whether you're exposed to a class environment and / or live in a Welsh-speaking area or not, there's always room for resources and other ideas that you can do on your own. My dad went through a stage of labelling everything in his house in Welsh at one point. It was bloody hilarious.

I once met a man from the London area who, when he moved to Wales, bought himself a Welsh dictionary as a sort of admission of being unable to attend classes but, at the very least, he was happy to show willing. He later gave said dictionary to me which, on a train journey to watch my beloved Wrexham AFC lift the LDV Vans Trophy in Cardiff's Millennium Stadium in 2005 (it was a three-hour train journey, what else was a 14-year-old boy going to do in all that time?), I had signed by Paul Burrell of English royalty and ITV's I'm a Celebrity Get Me Out Of Here fame. I hope he'd washed his hands after handling those cockroaches. But I digress.

My guess is that most people who make the decision to start learning Welsh will do exactly the same and grab a dictionary. In store or online, you'll usually find them under the 'foreign languages' sections. As much as this would probably be one of my first pieces of advice to anyone, there are obviously many things that a dictionary cannot do. Put it this way, even were you to learn every single word in a Welsh-English dictionary (compete with totally accurate spelling and pronunciation every time) you still wouldn't be fluent. A language is so much more than the individual words that make it and what a dictionary lacks – grammar, phrases, sayings etc – it cannot alone provide. If you're after a dictionary, I'd recommend *The Welsh Learner's Dictionary* by Heini Gruffudd. My copy that I received when I left primary school with my name printed inside it now resides on my bookshelf in a rather tatty and sorry state but without it, my life might have meandered a very different course. This book was my bible. Even today when I search for English to 'other language' dictionaries, I flick through the pages and base my choice on which one best resembles the layout of Heini's. *The Welsh Learner's Dictionary* not only offered words, but pages of handy notes including putting adjectives after nouns, how to mutate correctly and, most importantly, lists like *I am, you are, s/he is* and *I was, you were, s/he was*. It meant that, with a bit of patience, there wasn't much I was unable to express in Welsh so long as my dictionary was close to hand. With that book, I was fluent without even really trying. I loved it and I still do. Of all the novels and biographies, fictions, and non-fictions, I'd go as far as saying that it's one of my favourite books of all time. Diolch, Heini.

There are course books available in all different layouts and formats these days. *'Officially recognised by so-and-so'* in some, *'Best way to learn this-and-that'* in others. As I've already said, none of the enticing and eye-catching advertisements mean anything; it's all about what works best for you as an individual. Where the ocean of writers and companies win is that, initially, you might not yet be aware of what works best for you and so trying anything and everything is actually your best shot. From now on I offer no recommendations; after all the Welsh language isn't going to change from book to book. It's simply down to you to discover what works best.

As a young lad, I couldn't think of many worse things to do than read books. I didn't despise them; I often tried to pick up a book but would, for numerous reasons, always seem to leave them half-read or lose my way with them and give up. Perhaps that's why even now I prefer to read factual books that don't require me to follow a story, per se. It wasn't until I was around 19 when I read a book from start to finish in the space of around a fortnight (it was a great book) that I realised there was no shame in not enjoying reading – I simply hadn't yet found the right book for me. Now and again I still leave the odd book unfinished in between the many books I do actually finish. I liken it to something a friend, with whom I used to jam on acoustic guitars in his parents' garage, said to me of writing songs; *"I could write 20 songs and only one will be worth pursuing."* The point is to not stop trying... ever!

When mobile phones became more mainstream during my early teens, the question I'd most often hear was 'what can yours do?' Some had the timeless classic game Snake, and some let you choose your own ringtones and screensavers. These days, that question has been replaced by a cliché; "What *can't* your phone do?" There's an app for everything, right? In terms of learning languages, apps are brilliant – I honestly hold no punches in saying that. You can argue that seeing someone's head stuck in their phone makes them seem negative and less relatable but don't jump to conclusions too quickly. If you ever catch me with my head at a right angle to the rest of my body and my mobile phone demanding all my attention, I'm either blogging, tweeting, or learning languages. Just go to your app store and pop in the word '**Cymraeg**.' Before I eventually share some of my personal favourites, I bid you this advice; no matter how many hits you get when you search, download them all. Even the paid ones if you fancy it. Each will present you with a different path to the same goal. Often it can be the simplest and cheapest that are the best.

One such app I've been using for the past couple of years or so is ClozeMaster. When I opted for the paid version, I realised that I could pretty much get everything I needed with the free version – but I still pay regardless. I'm a nice guy! This clever app is super simple; you're presented with a sentence in English with the Welsh translation above but with a word missing. Below those you're given four Welsh words from which to choose with only one being the correct answer each time. If you use it correctly – ie don't just randomly guess (unless you have to) and definitely don't rush on without reading the completed sentences a few times afterwards to ensure total understanding – it's quite amazing how being exposed to completely random sentences can force your brain to do wonderful things with the language you already know. It even reads the sentence out for you afterwards. There are games where you can substitute your four options for a box where you have to type the missing word and even games where you will hear a sentence and must choose the word that's missing. It's not just for Welsh either. I'm currently using it with Gaelic, Breton, Irish, German, Latin and French too. *C'est magnifique.*

If you haven't heard of Duolingo then where have you been? This thing is revolutionary! Duolingo seems to be the go-to place to learn any language these days – from the big guns like Mandarin and Spanish to smaller languages like Icelandic and Welsh. There are more Irish and Scottish Gaelic learners completing the language on Duolingo than there are native speakers of the respective languages. You can even learn constructed languages like Klingon and Esperanto! Until Irish became available, I wasn't really a die-hard user. My passion was learning the Celtic languages and, in the early days of Duolingo, none were available. There were some decent apps knocking around for all six living Celtic tongues but nothing that offered the same experience as Duolingo eventually did. When Irish was finally added as the first Celtic language, my prior knowledge of Irish from the university meant I tore through the Emerald Isle's native language pretty swiftly; completing the tree (Duolingo's name for its courses) in a few months. Before I pushed onto reaching Level 5 in every strand and then onto the ultimate goal of becoming an illustrious Level 25 learner, I felt that each lesson brought me closer to competency. Just like in my youth when learning Welsh, I was becoming more and more capable of talking to myself in Irish when driving to work or out walking. Duolingo's clever tactic of repetition whether you get an answer correct or incorrect was forcing the language into my brain. Each lesson offered several listening games, translation games, word-matching games, missing word games and even speaking games; all of which encouraging the brain to take in vast amounts of language without even knowing it. Obviously doing Irish alone wasn't going to be enough for me so I broke my only-Celtic-languages rule and completed the German, French and Latin trees too. Scottish Gaelic was added on Saint Andrew's Day in 2019 and I spent pretty much the whole of that December getting to Level 5 in every lesson. I honestly put all of my positive interactions in French and German when visiting Bordeaux, Hamburg and Toronto in recent years totally down to Duolingo. It really works but, in order to see what the Duolingo experience was like with languages in which I had zero prior knowledge (often the case for people starting out in Welsh without having learnt Welsh in school), I recently started Polish too. The cleaners at my school, my Polish-speaking students and my maths-teaching, Slavic brother, Janek, are super impressed with how far I've come in such a short time. It's by far the hardest tree I've encountered (for the aforementioned reason of not having any prior knowledge in the language) but I know that time and effort will bring success.

Being invited to moderate for the Welsh course was a huge honour and, despite eventually only contributing around 3% of the course, I'm proud to say I was a part of something from which learners really do succeed in taking something. I still use Duolingo daily – mainly to keep plugging away at Irish. My daily streak is currently at over four years and I'll bet that if you ever bump into me at some point in the future and ask whether my streak is still going, I'll reply with any one of *'tá,' 'tha,' 'ja,' 'oui,' 'tak'* or *'ydy'*! Duolingo doesn't hold all the answers, but it'll give an incredible basis on which to bring your Welsh to life – especially if you manage to get every single strand up to Level 5 and keep them there.

As I mentioned earlier in the book, Aran Jones' Say Something in Welsh (SSIW) is another absolute winner and what's cool too is that the first few lessons are free. I've used it to learn Cornish and Manx Gaelic and, after having a go at the first 10 lessons a few times, I genuinely feel confident enough to speak these languages in the wild. I actually used the Manx I got from this course to speak to Adrian Cain, then the Manx Language Officer, on a visit to the Isle of Man. Aside from feeling immense pride that I could communicate in Manx with Adrian, it was mind-blowing to have him respond to me in near-perfect Welsh; himself having completed Aran's Welsh course a few weeks earlier.

Variety is the spice of life. Get me some cayenne pepper to add to my vegetable wraps and I feel like I've gone from recipe-book-chef to Michelin-star in a couple of sprinkles. In the same way, add extra salt to any of my food and I'll throw it at you. Some spices and additives work for us and some don't. Play around and hold fast to those that do work and put the others back on the shelf for other people. A dash of Duolingo here; a sprinkle of dictionary browsing there; all mixed in with signing up for Welsh classes and using whatever you already know out in the wild. Keep mixing your way to gourmet fluency. That was an awful analogy. Don't judge me!

# CYD-DESTUN
## *Context*

Even if you think it's too early for phrasebooks, it's not. Without wishing to make this book into just an extremely long-winded advertisement for Heini Gruffudd's publications, his *Learn Welsh Phrasebook and Grammar* is a really good one for learners. Another such phrasebook I acquired (and highly recommend) whilst completing my GCSEs was Leonard Hayes' *Welsh Phrases for Learners*. Whichever one you choose, they're great. Learners with minimal Welsh are immediately exposed to intricate ways the Welsh language expresses common ideas as well as receiving quick bites to use on the street as passing remarks or as additions to what you already have. For those with a decent understanding and basis in Welsh, peculiar phrases can be the steppingstone into shaping yourself into fluency.

The Manx language on the Isle of Man has seen somewhat of a revival in recent times. Aside from a multitude of fresh ideas, a large part of Manx's success is down to resources like *Manx Words* by James Harrison and Adrian Cain, which is based hugely on its Welsh predecessor, *Welsh Words* by Steve Morris and Paul Meara, and sells well on the island. The blurb on the back of *Manx Words* epitomises how phrasebooks in general can be a nice thing to simply browse without feeling the pressures of classes or speaking to strangers. "*Manx Words... provides a core vocabulary that will help learners to start using Manx in everyday situations.*" Presenting key vocabulary in context-orientated sections complete with grammar notes means if one was to sit and learn absolutely everything in it, one could quite easily be passed off as a fluent speaker even to native ears. Definitely the dog's b*****ks rather than the cat's tail! Get it?! And therein lies the point of keeping a decent phrasebook to hand. Look, cramming every phrase in a book into one's head isn't just time-consuming, it's nigh on impossible. I still open my copy of *Welsh Phrases for Learners* now and again and come across a beautiful saying I've never seen nor heard before – but each phrase one learns presents another opportunity to express oneself. Pick the right ones and you'd be easily mistaken for a native; at least in short interactions. Were my aim only to possess enough language to walk into my local café and order my brew from the Welsh speaking owner, three or four sentences would do. After all, it's unlikely I'll be discussing politics or moaning about the football to a busy barista, right?

Context is a huge deal in Welsh. Having such a comparatively small number of words is both a blessing and a hindrance to the language. It's believed that English has around four times the number of words than smaller languages like Welsh do. Welsh loses the ability to be as slick and as adaptable as languages like Spanish and English, but it means that when you learn a word you get more for your money, as it were. **Mawr** means *big* but it also means *large, grand, great* and a few others. Learning one word can mean you're able to create so many unique sentences without having to memorise a thesaurus. Couple these with a few stock phrases and you're away.

Don't get me wrong, it can be confusing. When you begin using your language socially as a learner, your brain is still taking necessary time to adapt to context. Fluent English speakers will hear a sentence like 'I'm feeling blue' and know exactly that someone's feeling down or sad. To English learners still tackling context, they might be forgiven for thinking that they're talking to a human-sized Smurf wannabe! It takes time but you'll get there. Just make sure your context is clear enough where using the words **rhiw** (*hill*) – where **rhyw**, pronounced the same way, means *sex* – and **gwaun** (*moor*) which, unless you're from the north west, is pronounced exactly the same as **gwain**; *vagina*! The latter of these two gems amplifies the sorely missed opportunity that the sign welcoming people to the town of Chirk near Wrexham (**Y Waun** in Welsh) doesn't read '*You are now entering Chirk.*' Lol*.

*Fun fact, **lol** means *nonsense* in Welsh. It's even included on the Wikipedia entry for the word. Yep, *lol* has a Wikipedia article.

# GÊM Y GYNHEDLAETH
*The Generation Game*

I fondly remember a game I played with a group of 12 and 13-year-olds when I was training in Rhosllannerchrugog. It's a game I've played a few times since too. The topic the regular class teacher had given me was to introduce the various ways of saying *'yes'* and *'no'* in Welsh. I'm sure the more mature readers will have already made the link between this mammoth task and the title of the section. I began with bringing a student to the front and challenged them to avoid using the words *'yes'* or *'no'* in response to some English questions I was about to pose to them. After we agreed as a class that avoiding these words was not an easy task for English speakers, I then dropped the bombshell that this is how Welsh – and many other languages – operate all the time. Amazed and confused, the lesson continued.

Nowadays, I often respond to those who take to posting on Welsh learners' social media groups worried about the multitude of ways to express *'yes'* and *'no'* in a similar manner to the how I respond to people worried about mutations or the gender of nouns; it takes time and they'll come naturally. I understand this isn't an easy thing to simply accept as a learner and I recognise how lots of people want to get their Welsh to nothing short of perfect before going out into the big wide world, but I would challenge any new learner to ask anyone who has learnt the language how they tackled it. My guess is they'll say they just got on with it and that it came with time and practise.

One day you'll hear a fluent speaker answer a question posed in, say, the past tense, with '**do**' or '**naddo**,' and you'll naturally make the connection yourself. If anything, this means of language acquisition is far more effective than destroying your brain looking over pages and pages of printed notes. I'm not saying anyone would be wrong to sit down and learn how to do it all properly, but I'll bet you'll find far more benefit in sitting down and learning various adjectives and verbs that truly are essential in conversation. One must also bear in mind that, in northern dialects, people will answer questions that include '**wedi**' in them with '**do**' or '**naddo**,' whereas southern speakers will answer them with '**ydw**' or '**nac/nag ydw**.' No book taught me this, I just learnt on the job. Then you've got northerners answering '**wyt ti eisiau...?**' (*do you want (a)...?*) questions with '**oes**' because that's actually what should be done. True story.

To put this whole question-answer headache into perspective, however many verbs there are in Welsh, that's how many ways there are to say '*yes*' and '*no*,' plus a few more. It's a bloody minefield and not something with which learners should be overly concerned, especially early on in the learning process. It certainly is not a prerequisite to plucking up the courage to go out and use the Welsh you have.

In the case of '*yes*' and '*no*,' there exists a cheat to cover the bases; **ie** (or **ia** in the north west and parts of the south east) for *yes* and **na(ge)** for *no*. Even natives regularly utilise these terms and no one bats an eyelid. In fact, I usually say *'aye'* these days when I want to say *'yes'* but that's just because I'm super cool, so the rest of you can't use that! Basically, **'ie'** and **'na'** do the job and they're more than good enough to be getting on with.

I'm often saddened when I hear of schemes of work in schools and colleges putting hours of emphasis on answering questions. For me it constitutes time taken away from learning real and living Welsh. Much like when I talk about mutations and noun genders, I often lead with advice along the lines of, if you're concerned and really want to know the ins and outs, learn to be aware of terms like **'ydw,'** **'naddo'** and **'oes'** before worrying about where you should be applying them yourself. Hear them and realise what they mean, but never feel pressured into thinking you're wrong to use **'ie'** and **'na'** when you're unsure.

My overall point here is to pick your battles. It's easier said than done, I understand – especially coming from someone who is a language teacher as well as a self-confessed amateur linguist. A great way of working out what you really need to learn is to start a diary or blog. This will give enable you to recognise how important certain parts of language are over others. It certainly helped me out and it's worth a try.

Cuddly toy, anyone? **Ie** or **na**?

# PAID AG YMDDIHEURO
## *Make no apologies*

When I was learning to play the guitar in my late teens, my uncle – who had already been learning the instrument himself – offered me a piece of advice that can be appropriated with ease to the learning of a language. Give it all you've got and let it become an extension of who you are. And then, at the times when it becomes too much and you can't take any more frustration, put it down and walk away. Knowing when to stop is just as important as knowing when to go at it. It's not worth growing a resentment – especially because of such honest means.

As a teacher of Irish who witnessed resentment from those entrusted to teach him the language in his own school days, Reuben Ó hAnluain believes he understands why such resentment existed. A great deal of the exacerbation displayed can be put down to a sort of defence mechanism to mask teachers' own insecurities and uncertainties deriving from their own struggles with the language. *"They didn't want students to ask questions,"* explains Reuben, *"so they created an atmosphere of fear."* Forging a resentment (especially as an educator) can turn people away from a language – often forever – and resenting one's own abilities by feeling the need to reach for the classic 'apology tactic' is one of the worst. Doing all we can to avoid it teaches us that we should never be afraid or insecure of admitting we're not perfect, and in addition, if you take nothing else from this book (hopefully you'll take much more, of course), let it be that learning a language in no way warrants any apology.

"*Sorry, my Welsh is pretty bad*" is a phrase I've used myself on many occasions and have since heard it from others multiple times more. Learners apologise well before they've even given themselves a chance to butcher the language, but *Sorry Speaker Syndrome* can extend all the way to those who many would define as fluent – even amongst those who now educate new learners. Many people are so quick to declare their ignorance of the language, even bragging about knowing no Welsh at all despite all the years of study in school. It really is just a self-defence safety net; it's infinitely easier to apologise for not believing one can speak a language than to try and speak it and go through the awkward process of trying to not make any mistakes. But times are changing. Even in my life I've noticed a shift between people claiming their language abilities are non-existent to nowadays admitting their Welsh is "*limited*" – despite both instances presenting the exact same capabilities in Welsh. There's now a pride in knowing some Welsh and it's spreading fast.

A while back I sent out a tweet that proclaimed that anyone who knew what '*good morning*' is in Welsh is, by my definition at least, bilingual. The responses were brilliant, but one in particular stood out as a debate starter. It was from a politician in south eastern Wales who replied that people using Welsh are "*wrong if we speak Welsh because we're being exclusive, and wrong if we don't because we're letting the language die!*" His additional hashtag read "*#cantwin*" [ie *can't win*]. It may seem that this hits the nail on the head at times, but it couldn't be further from the truth. Firstly, if someone accuses you of being exclusive, ignore them. Over 40% of the world is bilingual and only one in five have any knowledge of English. You wouldn't go to Austria and claim that German speakers were being 'exclusive,' would you?! Secondly, no one's "letting the language die." If Welsh does eventually become one of the thousands of languages expected to baseline on the operating table of communication by the end of the 20$^{th}$ century, then it will do so because of a multitude of reasons. That's not to say that residents of Wales are immune to the burden of our ancient tongue and every single person wishing to learn and use it are doing it the world of good, but one person can't be blamed for the death of a whole language and certainly no one's going to search you out personally as a bystander in the inquiry of why everyone in Wales only speaks English.

# DWYIEITHRWYDD I BAWB
*Bilingualism for all*

Mererid Hopwood, lecturer, poet, and the first woman to win the Chair at the National Eisteddfod in 2001 (yep, she's quite a big deal) claims that bilingualism must be treated as a spectrum – not as a binary ultimatum. Essentially, if you can say a few words in your target language, you're bilingual. Aside from being a heart-warming and confidence-encouraging theory, it's a tough one with which to argue on a pedagogical level too. Why would a Welsh-speaking café owner in Abersoch think they were dealing with anything other than another fluent speaker if they were asked "**Ga' i baned o goffi du a sgon, os gwelwch yn dda?**"

The ability to forge small interactions like these means it's then only down to building on them to bring yourself closer and closer to fluency. It's about forcing oneself to be in a position to learn whenever one can. For example, my new year's resolution a few years ago was to not scroll past any tweet or Facebook post that was in a language I was learning without at least trying to decipher its meaning first. I failed a few times and had to reach for a dictionary quite a bit, but those odd occasions I eventually understood even the gist made me so proud. It's like showing a simple Cornish phrase to a Welsh-speaker and watching their eyes widen with excitement when they realise they understood something that only a few thousand people on the planet admit they can comprehend.

My adult Welsh group asked me to create a WhatsApp group on which we still talk but after the first exciting few days of setting it up, there are often days that go by without any conversation whatsoever. Even so, we still chat fleetingly in Welsh between lessons and, as they often tell me, having the time to comprehend what's said – rather than having to constantly strain to pick up the gist of what can be lightning-paced native speakers – gives them a lot of confidence. Even if it's not quite as prominent as chatting in the street, how can using Welsh so freely in this way be classed as anything other than fluency to an outsider reading the conversation afterwards?

Learning anything takes commitment – and it will be difficult at times. I remember lying to my brother after we started going swimming in an attempt to get healthy stating that one week we wouldn't feel like going and we'd decide to leave it. If we were to then go back the week after we'd keep going for a long period of time, but if we didn't return, the idea of swimming our way to fitness would certainly fizzle out." Both ended up happening. Fine, this was just a ploy to try and manipulate him into coming swimming with me so I didn't have to go on my own, but I guess there's truth in it. Bringing ourselves to get back on the **ceffyl** when we inevitably fall off is a great trait to possess.

Learning a language isn't everyone's cup of tea, but that, in no way whatsoever means that only 'certain' people can succeed. Everyone *can* – just not everyone *does*!

# SYMUDWCH MEWN
*Move in*

At around the 75-minute mark at Wrexham AFC matches the match attendance is read out; first in Welsh and then in English. "***Y dorf swyddogol heddiw ydy….***" and then the number of bums on seats immediately follows. Aside from the '**heddiw**' (*today*), the above sentence isn't an easy one for non-fluent speakers to grasp. The words 'crowd' and 'official' aren't too often at the front of the queue for people to learn when they decide to take up the challenge of becoming competent in Welsh. Numbers, however, have been around most of us (especially those of us schooled in Wales) from a very early age. Now then, knowing that a ***mil**lennium* is a thousand years and a ***mil**lilitre* is one thousandth of a litre, my guess is that telling you that the word for a '*thousand*' in Welsh is '**mil**' will now probably stick in your head forever. You're welcome. Furthermore, armed with that word, I offer the following challenge to those who have a basic knowledge of Welsh numbers. Translate this: "***Y dorf swyddogol heddiw ydy* saith mil, pedwar cant ac wyth deg naw.**" Not too tough, right? *Seven thousand, four hundred and eighty-nine*. Going on the pretence that most supporters at Wrexham matches have at least some knowledge of numbers in Welsh, why do I hear only a smattering of claps from the crowd when the attendance is read out in Welsh but then a roaring applause from the whole stadium when it's read out in English? I fear that answering that question, despite its somewhat inevitable answer, might pain us all to the core.

I was teaching a lesson recently that encouraged the students to vary their adjectives when describing things. Their tendency is to stick to '**achos mae'n grêt**' (*because it's great*) when they're fond of something and '**achos mae'n ddiflas**' (*because it's boring*) when they're not so fond, so I attempted to tackle this. One particular task was to describe some pictures on the board. Up popped a snail. '**Bach**,' called a boy. *Small*. "**Pert**," offered a girl from the corner of the room. *Pretty*. "**Da iawn**," I said. "**Beth am ei chyflymder;** *speed* **ydy cyflymder?**" Blank faces watched my classroom-searching gaze. "*Well*," I pushed, "*is it fast?*" "*No!*" they giggly replied. "**Wel, beth 'te?**" – *Well, what then?* The blank faces continued. Even when I told them that the Welsh for '*slow*' is '**araf**,' it still took a good, few seconds for even one student to sheepishly ask whether that was the word that's on the roads. Yep, every single road in Wales that requires you to drive slowly. So every road in Wales, then! A similar occasion happened when a student asked me to translate the phrase '*I would like one.*' When I enquired as to how far they'd gotten in their head, they said "**hoffwn i**..." "*So, you just need to add* '*one*' *now then*" I replied. I kept to myself the fact that numbers are likely one of the first things children in English-medium schools learn of Welsh. Unfortunately, the student's brain seemed to want to make more work for itself by subconsciously convincing itself that '**un**' was just too simple and therefore couldn't be correct. But it *was* correct.

The Welsh language is alive around us with signs, announcements, official documentation, and advertisements not disguising that fact. But the eyes of the unwilling only seem to notice the word '*slow*' on our roads – not the *other* word above it. The unwilling ears switch off totally when Welsh is heard over a PA system at a football match or at a train station – even if the language is readily accessible when afforded a modicum of thought. Flick through TV channels and radio stations and you'll find yourself ready on the '*next channel*' button when you know a Welsh-language station like *S4C* or *Heart* is next up. The problem isn't that we dislike Welsh, the problem is that avoiding it is often already a part of our subconscious. Breaking out of such a habit is a monumental task but it can definitely be done. If you really want it, you have to let Welsh become your life and then live in it.

Put simply, we have every reason to be proud of however much Welsh we have. We always know enough to mean that, with a bit of effort, we'll frequently find at least something to understand if we're willing to listen and look out for it. Try listening to Welsh announcements at the train station and challenge yourself to understand them. If you struggle, rest assured the English is about to follow. Read the Welsh side of documents or letters you receive and once again rest assured that your English safety net is ready on the other side. Use a cashpoint in Welsh; if you get to a point where you think you're about to withdraw £300 rather than £30 and don't know how to stop it, just press *cancel* and try again in English. More important than all these little challenges you set for yourself, give your everything to become conscious of the Welsh around you.

When you start to learn Welsh, you make a sacrifice to embark on a full-on quest. You know you'll rarely feel what native speakers feel, but you take up the task of passing it on to others so that they can feel it. Learning Welsh, especially as an adult, is a sacrifice that also bears a burden. Learners must be prepared for both these things and strive to fulfil and respect them. At the beginning of this chapter I implored you to seek out your cause and your reason for learning Welsh. As I said, you probably already have one even if sometimes it takes a little time and thought to actually realise and articulate it. Whatever your reason is, you must also add to it the 'burden clause,' as I refer to it. Whether you like it or not, I'm afraid. If you're willing to accept that your reason for learning Welsh is no longer simply 'to be respectful of where I call home' or 'to help me with my job' or 'to speak to my children in our native language,' but it's now your reason *plus* the burden that is bestowed upon you by this language, then you are already of appropriate mindset to become a speaker. If not, and it seriously pains me to say it, but Welsh might not be for you.

Whether any of the tactics, techniques and motivational words work for you in your quest to learn Welsh or not, there's always the ever reliable, intoxicating cold pint of Wrexham Lager option to fall back on to get you speaking Welsh… or what might sound like Welsh, anyway!

# PENNOD 4
# PAM LAI'R DDWY? – Why not both?

## DWY AM BRIS UN OND OES LLE AMDANYNT?
*Two for the price of one but is there room for both?*

To whatever extent my theory (that I'll discuss in the final chapter of this book) about the English language having been 'highjacked' is true, I genuinely mean it when I said I'm super glad that I can command the English language to the level I can. This is from someone who has witnessed first-hand the destruction – however intentional and / or unintentional – that a larger language can have on smaller ones around it. But can there not be a place for both English and Welsh in modern society? After all, with our dragon's tail the same shape as its tongue, it's no wonder they say **mae gan y ddraig ddwy dafod** – *the dragon has two tongues*.

Essentially, I'm in no way advocating the abandoning of English. That would be madness. It's one of the most important languages on the planet – if not *the* most important – and a language in which all inhabitants in Wales are already fluent. Rivalries aside, it doesn't matter whether our neighbours' language has been a symbol of oppression for centuries or whether it simply turned up yesterday and most of the planet just started using it; we have it. No one is denying it and nor should anyone bemoan it. Everything we then have through our own native language is in addition to our utilisation of English. I task anyone to come up with a drawback of that.

So where do minority languages fit into this? In a lecture about his own nation's quest to be bilingual, Seán Ó Riada explains how the English and Irish languages were *"utterly incompatible. English sounds derive from the roof of the mouth, suggesting control and authority. This is why is it easier to lie in English"* he said. *"Irish, however, came from deeper down – like the sounds made by a Tibetan monk;* ummmming *from the chest. It is easier to pray in Irish."* Of Welsh, creator of several Elven languages with huge grammatical and orthographical similarities to Welsh and one-time lecturer of Middle Welsh at Cambridge university, JRR Tolkien once referred to Wales' native tongue as the *"senior language of the men of Britain."* He was, of course, referring to a Britain now lost, but the sentiment to the language certainly remains. He speaks of a people who forged these islands to become a beacon of prosperity in harsher times using a language we now know as Welsh. Now imagine being in possession of both the world's global tongue *and* a language considered so highly by one of the greatest writers (and indeed minds) of the twentieth century. *"And,"* Tolkien added, *"Welsh is beautiful."*

At times, however, the world is not beautiful. Sometimes beauty takes a backseat to driving forward in the name of progress – whether we like it or not. Going back to Ireland where Michael Hartnett, an Irish poet, pursued the dream of a bilingual state in which English would be the language of trade and commerce claiming it's *"a great language to sell pigs in."* Irish, in Hartnett's mind, was to preside over matters of philosophy, love and poetry. This dilemma plagues me more than most others when I ponder the future of Welsh. Could it be conceivable to have *every* school in Wales teaching science and business through English, with the likes of history, religious studies and the arts through Welsh – the way our language *should* be used – or do we maintain the status quo of a largely English-medium schooling provision across the country? If we pursue the former, we might then confine words like **'disgyrchiant'** and **'ffrithiant'** (*gravity* and *friction* respectively) to forgotten dictionaries, but also open our minds to arts and culture through a medium in which people have pondered the same matters for generations previous. We'd have a populous fluent in English for business, science, and commerce and fluent in Welsh for music, community, and ideology. In a way it's already beginning to happen. Go to any livestock market in west Wales and you'll hear Welsh chit-chat everywhere, except for when the auctioneer conducts the lightning-fast bidding. Is this the place for Welsh, and indeed English, in a modern Wales?

But, like we always do, we find ourselves playing off the pros and cons of English and Welsh against one another. Surely this doesn't have to be the case. Don't believe the fakery either; learning or possessing another language does not mean your native tongue will suffer. In fact, my English has only gone from strength to strength since my early 20s – coincidentally around the same time I abandoned my **dysgwr y Gymraeg** (*Welsh learner*) tag. The fact is I've been more conscious of grammatical correctness and have better understood the unique and complex syntactical peculiarities of English simply because of my experiences in encouraging my brain to learn a different language, rather than merely acquire one from birth. Without the process of learning Welsh, I'd probably never have come across terminology like *prepositions*, *adverbial clauses* and *personal pronouns*. To aid in proving my point, it was Geoffrey Willans who said; *"You can never understand one language until you understand at least two."* Finally, to unashamedly lower myself to a patronising concoction of arrogance and ignorance, I find that those who claim knowing these intricacies as trivial are the same people who regimentally 'forget' to use apostrophes and believe that raising one's voice makes you better understood.

Learning new languages certainly enhances your brain – it most definitely does not hinder it. Besides, one more positive to keep in mind when acquiring Welsh is that our beautiful Celtic languages are stored in the heart, not the mind.

# CREU LLE
*Creating a place*

When asked about language skills, one often hears the same question: "Do you *speak* it?" Well, in the case of blanket-covering every individual in Wales; no, most of us don't. However, we all *know* Welsh. As I argued in the previous chapter, whether one is totally fluent or only knows how to count to ten, we are *all* bilingual in Wales. Sadly, no one ever asks whether we '*know*' a language. If they did, most of us would definitely reply with a resounding "Yes."

But true fluency is not simply the knowledge *of* another language. One might have the ability to understand many languages, but in the eyes of those who stand fast to the notion that a language only lives when it is actually *used*, it's open for questioning whether these people are truly bi/multilingual. *Knowing* must eventually become *speaking* and *using*, and our job is to find that use for Welsh – to find a *place* for Welsh.

By a *place* I do not refer to a particular location (ie a sort of reservation as found in the Americas), I suggest a time and a space. From a passing moment, to weeks on end; from afternoons in your living room, to the hustle and bustle moments of city life. When I go to watch the mighty Wrexham AFC, I can't use my Welsh. There's no ban on it, of course – in fact, the club have made it their policy in recent years to provide all stadium announcements bilingually. I just don't feel comfortable using it at the match. Neither can I get myself to use the language in the heat of our weekly staff 5-a-side football games. Being fluent means that I know exactly *how* to scream at a winger to cross the ball in or command midfielders to help out a creaking defensive line, but I can't seem to ever actually utter those words in Welsh. It's as if my brain forgets I can speak Welsh in just those split-second moments. Perhaps it's that my learner-mind won't work quickly enough to keep up with football's lightning pace or perhaps I'm just not *meant* to talk football in my second language. On the flip side, I'd never contemplate texting my Welsh-speaking friends in English – about football or otherwise. I wouldn't talk to my cat in English and, should I ever be lucky enough to have children, the only other language I'll speak with them after Welsh will be another Celtic language. If you're willing to search for them or, in some cases, even brave enough to forge them yourself, there can be a *place* for every language you speak or learn. What's more, our 'Welsh places' can be anywhere and everywhere and even different for each one of us. Whether our Welsh is for talking to our pets, for lazy Sunday mornings or for discussing the shopping list, it doesn't matter. Give it a place.

When I first realised that Welsh required a living place in my life, a few years ago I made myself a promise. I promised to never say the word '*thanks*' (or any variation of it) again. Think of it as a New *Life* Resolution. A simple idea that has yielded the most wondrous of outcomes. From people asking impromptu questions about the Welsh language or simply smiling back with a '*thank you,*' to people – fluent or not – replying with a '**diolch**' of their own and even a '**croeso**' here and there. The guys on the turnstiles at Wrexham's Racecourse ground always greet me with a **diolch** when I thank them for scanning my ticket and returning it back to me. I've even had the odd person say '**Www, ti'n siarad Cymraeg?**' and chatted about anything and nothing at all; random people forging a conversation simply because of their ability to speak another language. I've found Welsh speakers in my own village who I never knew even spoke it simply because they heard me say that one word. And to those of us not yet fluent who are perhaps thinking of making this change themselves, don't be put off by Welsh speakers suddenly hurtling their Cymraeg at you at 143 miles per hour; just tell them in English what you're doing and see if you can get them to denounce their own use of *'thanks'* themselves. In short, use your manners; DON'T say *thank you*!

Should you not feel confident enough to give your language a verbal place, why not use it in written form as a start? One should never disregard the written word in the quest for fluency in other languages. Write **Nadolig Llawen** on your Christmas cards, write addresses in Welsh on letters and post **Pen-blwydd Hapus** on your friends' Facebook profile to help them celebrate their special day. My non-fluent dad does it all the time, **chwarae teg**. My own journey to becoming *líofa as Gaeilge* (*fluent in Irish*) has led me to tweeting, blogging, and even writing articles for magazines in the language. I suppose these are my 'Irish places.' It's the desire to say what you want to say – disregarding inevitable mistakes – and smiling when you achieve it. Forcing yourself to not give up and to use any means necessary to express what you want to express. Ironically, using a language in this more permanent and wide-reaching fashion can sometimes do more good than the odd '*bore da*' to mere individuals at work or on the street. Another idea for the *non-verbal* Welsh crew is to grab a novel – there are plenty out there these days that are especially for learners or those who wish to reconnect with the language. You'll find plenty with '*Nofel i ddysgwyr*' emblazoned proudly across the front. These offer more of an *adult* storyline than simply picking up a Welsh book for young teenagers – even though they'd both contain the same sort of language. No excuses!

The only unfortunate part of making a place for our sapling Welsh skills is the fact that, especially in eastern areas, the place we make for the language can often be the only time we ever encounter it. Being described by people from other countries as being a 'welcoming' and 'tolerant' people may well be a badge of honour in an increasingly distant world, but cynics argue that it simply derives from the fact we were far too willing to give up speaking Welsh with visitors and, eventually, with people who moved to Wales to live. This has subsequently led to a modern condition where we just punt for English straight away, instead of giving our Welsh a chance. Encouraging our already-fluent speakers to start every conversation in Welsh (or at least make it explicitly clear to others that they speak Welsh and are open to switching to it) can and will make an incredible difference for learners as well as for people who wrongly believe the language is dying. So why doesn't it happen?

# DEIFIO MEWN I'R PEN DWFN
## *Headfirst into the deep end*

How do children acquire language from their parent(s)? They just seem to hear it, repeat what they can when they think it's appropriate and straight up ignore anything they don't understand. As adults, we can see how the morals of these tactics don't quite marry up with how we live our grown-up lives, as much as ignorance can most certainly be bliss at times! In the previous section I mentioned how giving Welsh a place via the odd sentence or post on social media can edge us into using what we can and being proud of it. This is all well and good, but it's got nothing on diving in headfirst.

Not so long ago I was watching a clip of Liverpool manager, Jürgen Klopp, take on a young lad to guess football teams from only the flags of the players' nationalities placed in each player's position. The clip was entirely in German and, although I didn't understand every word, I still found myself subconsciously saying *'nein'* when I knew one of the answers given was incorrect. My German was nowhere near good enough to explain *why* the answer was incorrect, but the fact the German word for *'no'* just slipped out was intriguing. Language flows out when we're surrounded by it.

Usually reserved for young people to practise their Welsh, Glan-llyn isn't exclusive to learners. Much like it's counterparts in Llangrannog and Cardiff Bay, the Urdd camp in Y Bala is a great place to immerse oneself in Welsh. Nant Gwrtheyrn on Pen Llŷn operates in a similar way too but is more exclusively for adults.

We take students every year to Glan-llyn and it's a wonderful chance for us as teachers to use living Welsh with students rather than the classroom Welsh they're so used to hearing (and often ignoring). Going back there reminds me of my own time visiting as a student and of how my own Welsh improved exponentially by throwing myself into the depths of the language. One such memory I have is of Ifor ap Glyn giving us a talk on how to appreciate Welsh literature for our A Level studies back in 2005. The poet, presenter and currently serving National Poet of Wales since 2006, gave a wonderful speech and welcomed students to stay behind afterwards for any questions. Mine was simple; 'Ga' i'ch llofnod, os gwelwch yn dda?' (*Can I have your autograph, please?*). He happily obliged and we got talking about my interests. I told him I'd recently discovered the Celtic languages and he showed me how words beginning with *p-* sounds in Welsh, Cornish and Breton often started with a *c-/k-* sound in the three Gaelic languages; a fact I'd letter come to fully comprehend as my knowledge of the Celtic languages increased. Before leaving, he told me about a show he had coming up on S4C called *'Popeth yn Gymraeg'* (*Everything in Welsh*) which saw him travel around Wales attempting to speak nothing but Welsh. Spoiler alert; he managed it, but struggled in more eastern areas of the country. As a side note, I've been meaning to ask him after all these years about the poem he told on the streets of Wrexham during his series that included the name of my home village, Leeswood.

In 2007, Irish writer, traveller and television producer, Manchán Magan, embarked on a similar mission for Irish language channel, TG4, whereby he visited the four provinces of Ireland in search of the language his grandmother learnt and taught him. In his article entitled '*Cá Bhfuil Na Gaeilgeoirí?*' (*Where Are All The Irish Speakers?*) for The Guardian newspaper in January 2007, Manchán asks; "*Should we stick a do-not-resuscitate sign around its neck and unplug the machine, or else get over our silly inferiority complex and start using the bloody thing?*"

The aim for both Ifor and Manchán was clearly to gauge how much of their respective nations' native languages were still around, but what stood out for me was how non-speakers actually understood much of what they were saying – with a bit of encouragement at times, of course. When faced with a challenge, as humans we often rise to it. As much as having the opportunity to throw oneself unreservedly into Welsh relies largely on where and around whom one lives, it's not entirely *exclusive* to these situations. It's no doubt the most optimistic of ways to acquire a language, but with the correct mindset and a desire to seek out the opportunities to make it work, I don't doubt that any learner's brain will quickly start to reach for Welsh before English – even if it's just shouting '*na*' at silly YouTube clips at first!

# TYNNU'N HUNAIN LAWR
*Putting ourselves down*

Gaining any experience in any given field absolutely ruins your view on it – fact. Allow me to explain.

We bemoan doctors and nurses when we're sat in a hospital waiting room for four hours when, in truth, most of us would happily sit through twice that time if hospital walls were transparent and we could see how busy medical staff actually are. Moan about a tea-sipping ground worker like my brother for not getting on with his job only to later find out that he was simply taking a well-earned 15-minute pause for a prerequisite job to be completed before continuing. The truth is, until we truly live something, we haven't got a bloody clue. Walk a mile, and all that.

However, when working my way through my Welsh degree, I went through a phase of which I'm not at all proud but, in all honesty, I couldn't prevent. Every time I'd read or hear anything in Welsh, rather than be grateful of my newly acquired fluency, I'd scrutinise… even to the point where I'd read swathes of text in Welsh and would afterwards be able to recall the two occasions of mis-mutation but remember absolutely nothing of the important part – it's actual content. If I'm totally honest, this still happens even now but today I'm glad that wisdom has steered me in such a way as to overlook trivial, grammatical imperfections and be proud that someone has used the language that *I'm* proud I can understand. I'm the second type of purist – I'll describe the first type later. I'm the one who appreciates and believes in the beauty of truly 'correct' Welsh, but also appreciates and believes in the encouragement and celebration of any occasion our language is utilised.

We've all seen those images shared on social media displaying, for example, a page full of the number 8 and you're challenged to find the single letter S. You search and search for far longer than you should but, as soon as you find it, you can't ever un-see it. Look away and back again, your eyes fall straight back onto that letter S. That's like what happens when your Welsh (or indeed any language) reaches a level that, in all honesty, is nothing short of 'unnatural'. Any spelling mistake on a poster or mis-mutation in a formal letter and, no matter how hard you try, your eyes are drawn back to it – craving some *Tippex* or a red marker pen. Other correction fluids and coloured writing implements are available! But we're meant to make mistakes. My guess is that many of the irregular verbs and grammatical exceptions in all languages derive from some sort of miscommunication or misunderstanding. Languages evolve for many reasons – it just so happens that one of those reasons is imperfections. It took me years to realise and accept this fact.

For all their love for the language, the first type of purist are those who are often quick to pounce on any and all 'incorrect' Welsh. In stark contrast, most grammar nuts in English spotting misuse of their language simply roll their eyes and move on. Despite language misuse being a tad annoying, I totally understand that the English language is richly used enough to not suffer if someone writes *your* when they really meant *you're*. Welsh, on the other hand, does not enjoy as wide a usage as English to possess such levels of arrogance. Do you remember when everyone kicked off in uproar and the whole world went into meltdown about the signs in supermarkets that read '*10 items or less*' when they should have read '*10 items or fewer*'? No, neither do I!

A few years ago, a group was set up on Facebook called 'Arwyddion Cymraeg Gwael' (*Appalling Welsh Signs*) which followed a similar pattern to two books released a year or so prior entitled Sgymraeg (an amalgamation of the words *scummy* and *Cymraeg*) and Sgymraeg 2. With the Facebook group becoming a sort of live continuation of the books, both platforms poked fun at signage and other displays of the Welsh language that were nothing short of laughable. Initially, signage that told pedestrians in English to safely walk on the right-hand side of the road whilst urging Welsh speakers to walk into oncoming traffic on the left (my theory is they were trying to kill us Welsh speakers off!) did the rounds and received viral fame in Welsh-speaking social media circles. Others included Welsh translations of directions like '*Cyclists Dismount*' as '*Bladder Inflammation Dismount*', but one of the most famous was a sign on a Swansea roundabout that, in English, told HGVs to use an alternate route with the Welsh translation explaining how someone [the translator] was not in the office at the moment but any translations would be completed as soon as possible.

Over time, as misspellings and forgotten mutations became the butt of many a joke in Welsh speaking circles, sign makers across the country finally began to take the hint and realised that online translation engines and automated email responses were less than appropriate for public signage. But as official signage became more and more correct, native speaking small business owners etc were still promoting their own stuff using their own colloquial Welsh. For groups like 'Arwyddion Cymraeg Gwael', correct official signage meant there was no longer much else at whom its members could poke fun than the native speakers who were sometimes making honest (yet less bewildering) mistakes when producing their own bilingual displays. Clearly, in the eyes of first-order purists, their mistakes were mistakes nonetheless and were, ultimately, free game on which to pick.

In turn, the sharing of images like these sparked heated debates. On the one side were people who believed that all users of Welsh have a duty to ensure correctness in their visual correspondence, and on the other side – where I firmly and proudly placed myself – were those who believed that people giving Welsh a try was a victory for the language whether it was totally 'correct' or not. Official signage displaying a Google Translate monstrosity I'm willing to laugh at, but not an honest mistake like forgetting a noun is feminine that might just put off a native speaker from using their language ever again. It's not unheard of. In some cases, it was obvious from the pictures shared on the group's page that these were local businesses and everyday users of Welsh who, with perhaps a lack of confidence to use their Welsh anyway, were making the effort to ensure our language maintained its place in the eye of those who call Wales their home.

Whether it's our first language or our eighth, we'll sometimes get stuff really wrong. We're meant to – much like the typos I've inevitably missed when editing this book. I once went to Brittany greeting people with '**Kenavo**,' only later realising that was the word for *goodbye*. Looking back, I remember those Breton faces as an interesting mixture of *'what?'* and *'aww, he's trying, bless him!'* Honestly, I'm sure both myself and my Sant Maloù *victims* often think of this giant muck up and have a giggle about it. It's part and parcel of learning and using language. Part and parcel of life in general.

Whether you believe that my side of the argument as a second-order purist possesses the moral high ground or not, I've learnt that encouraging Welsh (in any condition) was indeed a victory for our endangered tongue whose yet-to-flower buds still suffer from their over-weening neighbour-language. If there's any language on the planet that can suffer a degree of erosion and notice nigh on zero effects, it's unfortunately not Welsh.

# SIARAD 'GOOD ENGLAND'
*Speaking 'good England'*

I was 29 years old when I discovered the difference between verbs like '*drank*' and '*drunk*,' '*went*' and '*gone*,' and '*spoke*' and '*spoken*.' Of course, the second word in each pairing is actually a past participle; not strictly speaking a verb. If you're interested, the past participle version is always coupled with '*have*' or '*had*' which, when used in this manner, become known as auxiliary verbs. There are millions of English speakers across the globe who've never heard of a past participle. There are millions who don't know (and probably don't care) what the difference is between them and simple past tense verbs. There are millions who just punt for whichever one they want and then get on with life. No one questions their choice and certainly no one ever revokes their status as an English speaker. So, what's my point?

Well, there's a sad irony surrounding people who, despite having even had a Welsh-medium education or a Welsh-speaking background, bemoan their own Welsh ability. Even worse can be the fact they often don't spot the sea of mistakes in things they write and say in English; including the occasional misuse of a past participle! This isn't me being pedantic – even though I very often can be. It's me realising that, for some reason, it appears socially acceptable to have sloppy English but not sloppy Welsh. This is more a problem with society at large rather than with any individual but it really needs to be tackled.

**Is fearr Gaeilge briste na Béarla cliste** (*Better broken Irish than clever English*) was a saying I paraphrased on a hoodie I had made while in university where I substituted *Gaeilge* for *Breatnais* (Irish for *Cymraeg*). I later also saw our own version the phrase; **Gwell Cymraeg slac na Saesneg slic** – *Better slack Welsh than slick English*. Both epitomised how we need to rid ourselves of any pressure to be masters of the language(s) we learn. Just because one has never heard of the Oxford comma or the subjunctive mood, doesn't mean one should question their English fluency, right?

No matter the eventual grammatical state of the Welsh you're willing to use, I offer you one other saying that I regularly hear from Irish speakers: **Gaeilge mas féidir, Bearla mas gá**. In Welsh; **Cymraeg os gelli di, Saesneg os oes raid**. *Irish/Welsh if you can, English if you must*. People will tell you that Welsh is a difficult language. In truth, it's not exclusively Welsh; it's that all languages can be difficult – end of. I mean, Imagine having to learn English from scratch. For example, to express *walk* in the past tense we say *walked*, just like *talk* becomes *talked*. So, *run* becomes *runned*, right? Wait, what the hell is *ran*? Does *win* become *winned*? What? *Won*? Why not *wan*? The past tense of *go* is *goed* though, right? Wait, it's WHAT?! And that's just looking at a few verbs in the past tense. It's reckoned that English has over 100 irregular verbs where Welsh has less than a quarter of that number. Native Welsh speakers learn English quickly enough but hardly any of them would claim to be linguists. It's not Welsh itself that's notoriously difficult, it's merely that the learner may not be applying their energies into effective enough places to acquire the language and, perhaps worse still, are worried that they're not ready to use their target language until they're just as proficient as they are in their mother tongue. It's all about encouraging, and even forcing oneself, to experience as much exposure in the language as possible and to lose any inhibitions and feelings of insecurity. **Haws d'eud na 'neud**, of course – *easier said than done*. Essentially, forget you're learning it in order to be learning it. Just, ya know, do it and be proud of yourself.

# Y CYMRY O BLAID Y CYMRY
*The Welsh helping the Welsh*

When they spot a stumbling learner, native Welsh speakers do one of four things; 1) turn to English to save time, 2) turn to English to prove they also speak good English, 3) wait for the learner to finish then fire off 100mph colloquial dialect back at them or, 4) wait for the learner to finish and then think up an appropriate way to respond in Welsh.

I'd love to say that these four instances each enjoy even a fair 25% of situations but, alas, I doubt that's the case. The latter (and better) option enjoys by far the least airtime, of course. Few people have the time these days to wait around for stutterers – especially when native Welsh speakers possess perfectly good English. In these instances, Welsh is therefore kept exclusively for native speakers – a bold move by speakers of a language predicted to be one of the 6,000+ global languages to perish by the end of the current century.

We need two things to combat this problem and the first is time. Are we really in such a rush *all* the time? In a fast-paced world, sometimes all we really need is a moment to take off our shoes, relax, and let our souls catch up with us. Time is a healer as well as a giver and we should never underestimate that. The second problem is that there's a huge lack of much needed quick-fix tips and ideas for fluent speakers to help learners. It's unbelievably saddening to think of vast number of native speakers I've known whose partners / friends / colleagues have asked them to use Welsh with them and then found that, often after just a couple of sentences, the potential learner has retracted their request on the basis that they found learning with a native speaker too difficult.

The burden of sharing the language belongs to every speaker and it must be done correctly – especially when people are essentially begging us to help them learn. A poll in 2019 stated that nearly 7 in every 10 non-Welsh-speakers in Wales wished they could learn or had paid more attention in school when they had the chance. Not that where someone is born matters in this debate but considering around 70% of the population are Welsh born, we can confidently presume that the number of those with a birth link to Wales wishing to acquire the language can't be far off 100%. How many of them are coming to us asking for help and, through genuinely no fault of our own as fluent speakers, we're putting them off? Perhaps their Welsh lessons in school put them off and they were hoping for better luck on their own outside of the education environment. Suddenly, native speakers are crushed with an insane amount of pressure.

# DYGWCH FEICHIAU EICH GILYDD
*Share eachother's burdens*

In mid-2020, S4C broadcast a 5-part series following five non-native Welsh speakers' journeys to learning Welsh. Sponsored by *learnwelsh.cymru* and narrated by Alex Jones, *Iaith ar Daith* (*The Language on a Journey*) saw one celebrity each week join up with a Welsh-speaking celebrity friend with the aim of completing challenges over a three day period. Coupled with only the knowledge they may (or may not) have had from their English-medium school and one full day learning Welsh with the fantastic *Say Something in Welsh* course, off they went to use their skills in the wild. Of course, showing celebrities' successes and shortcomings throughout the learning process is a great way of encouraging those still trying to shift their '*dysgwr/aig*' tag but, as a teacher, I noticed something else. With the utmost respect and admiration to the mother-tongue buddies, it was clear that, through no fault of their own, most had little or no idea of how to impart the language effectively. Many were often too quick to use English or impatient in waiting for the end of a stumbling Welsh sentence.

This is in no way a remark towards their language skills – their Welsh was perfect. Nor is this an attempt to patronise those who haven't been trained to teach languages. For me, the whole series was littered with odd occasions where the imparting and sharing of the language wasn't as effective as it could have been. It struck me that this must be the case with most families and friend circles where perhaps only one person speaks Welsh.

As I pondered in the previous section, how many people have told their partner or friend that they want to learn Welsh but have ended up letting it fizzle out over time or even had a bit of a barney over the learning process and never spoke of it again? Teaching and learning require a concoction of factors such as patience, encouragement, opportunity, time, ability, understanding, empathy and many more. Unfortunately for those imparting or receiving the language, missing just one of these factors can halt the whole process; a bit like removing any one of oxygen, fuel or a spark from the act of making a fire. Perhaps Welsh-medium schools could begin to offer enrichment or pastoral lessons a few times throughout their students' school careers that arm young people with skills and ideas for how to deal positively with the inevitable occurrence of someone, at some point in their lives, urging them to teach them Welsh; be it just a sentence or the entire language. At the very least, students' skills in communication and in dealing with others would be better for it. Furthermore, it's reckoned that only 46% of families where only one parent speaks Welsh pass on the language to their child(ren). Disregarding the education sector and its successes in maintaining the numbers of Welsh speakers for a moment, this percentage is worrying and would almost certainly, being below 50%, eventually lead to the demise of the language.

## BETH DDYLWN I WNEUD FELLY?
*What should I do then?*

It's become clear to me since collating this chapter that the task of the native speaker as a 'teacher' is just as mammoth as the learner's task of acquiring a whole language. Either way, there are ways we can crash-course ourselves into helping others and/or training ourselves how to be patient with one another.

It starts with a willingness. I've tried for years to have my wife let me teach her some Irish but to no avail. I'm hugely annoying so clearly I'll keep trying until she breaks but, however heartbreaking, it's not up to us as teachers to bring out their language if our learners don't want to. There are, of course, ways and means via subtleties to encourage our learners to give it a shot. Planting the seed of a language isn't a crime, right? Encourage them to learn and be confident enough to tell them that you're happy to be a part of their journey.

If that day does arrive and you're asked to become someone's teacher, the first thing to establish is why they've decided to do it. Praise any reason behind wanting to better themselves linguistically and let them know you're with them every step of the way. Tell them what you personally like about being bilingual and how it's helped you or changed you somehow. Let them know that you're there as another resource in a sea of apps, books, music, games, radio, TV, road signs, adult classes, etc that will eventually bring them into the world of fluency.

A common occurrence often falling on the ears of fluent speakers when their family and friends take up learning Welsh is the question "*What does* [Welsh word/phrase] *mean?*" The simple avenue out of this is to provide the student with their answer and move on. While this is by no means a poor choice, imploring the learner to take a shot at it themselves can be of greater benefit. "*No, what do YOU think it means?*" or "*No, how do YOU think it's said?*" As teachers we'll always have the answer on which we can fall back, but, coupled with reminding the learner of the troublesome sentence maybe an hour-or-so later, the chances of the word or phrase's eventual acquisition is greatly increased.

Learning any skill requires brain pain; you can't become an expert at something using YouTube tutorials alone. Learning, like any form of wisdom, requires education *and* experience... with a sprinkling of effort and enthusiasm. Our job as teachers is to provide the experience as well as the education in equal measure – never simply 'listen to me and you'll get it.'

I recently posted a challenge on social media for Welsh learners with the aim of testing out an idea I had for use with my own students. The challenge asked learners to find out information about me that I'd posted in English (my cat's name, my dominant hand, my least favourite food etc) by any means necessary. Some questions posed had misplaced words and mutations and some involved information about themselves plus '**a ti?**' (*and you?*) at the end... cheeky! Some asked a number of questions to yield an answer and some used only a single word. What made me smile was the fact that, despite the linguistic 'hiccups,' I was able to totally understand and respond to each and every demand and provide the information for which they were looking. The learning had been passed to the learners who were forced to use only the language they had which, in truth, is similar to how we acquire language as children. Many who attempted the challenge were later able to notice gaps in their language and knew exactly how their dictionaries could help them – rather than browsing them for no reason. It also gave me the opportunity to offer some grammatical pointers that are seldom found in dictionaries. They'd clearly already done the 'education' part, providing an outlet for the 'experience' element was all that was required.

Undoubtedly, and as I mentioned earlier, our job as teachers is a tough one – especially if we're not trained to do it in the first place. Be your learner's perseverance and **daliwch ati**.

# DEWIS DY FRWYDRAU
*Picking your battles*

There's a fine line between speaking slowly enough for a learner to understand you, and too slowly to make them feel patronised and put off. Of course, it's all about knowing your learner and making it clear from the off that patronising really isn't your intention. Think about the phrases you're confident they know and speed those up a bit.

Should the learner say something that isn't 'correct' *per se*, the 'teacher' in this situation must make an immediate decision. Much like the subconscious desire to turn your steering wheel away from an icy skid on the road – don't do that, by the way! – the temptation is to correct learners straight away. As Scott Quinnell, one of the celebrities on S4C's *Iaith ar Daith* said; *"I've got a lot of friends who speak Welsh, and I've got a lot of friends who speak Welsh to me. I've tried in the past [to speak Welsh back to them] then people who do speak Welsh speak it very very well will try to... and I don't think they do it to be awkward or anything... they'll stop you and every word that you say wrong, they'll put you right. So, in the end you just don't say anything."* As it turned out, Quinnell's Welsh was incredible – so good that he completed the whole 3-day challenge (including an interview for S4C's evening magazine show, *Heno*) using nothing but Welsh. To think that even someone with such ability in the language has for years held the view that speaking Welsh isn't worth it, we must also carefully consider how total beginners feel too.

Correct learners once too many and we run the risk of turning them away; so much so that they may never come back. If a mutation is missed, is that truly worth noting? If they say **gweld** (*to see*) instead of **gwylio / watsiad** (*to watch*), does it really matter? Something I try with non-speakers of Welsh is the '*that'll do + smile*' response. It shows that a learner's response is good enough (which it usually is), but also suggests there's room for improvement. Those really pushing themselves with Welsh will usually ask how they can improve it straight away, whereas those to whom we might refer as 'fleeting learners' get to be praised for giving their Welsh a try but aren't then bombarded with heaps of grammar that will probably put them off in the long run. The '*+ smile*' bit is just there just because I'm a nice guy! In other words, if you understood them (and you reckon others would too), leave it and move on. At the end of the day, it's your call.

Doing this multiple times per day can be stressful and tedious, but what is language acquisition if not just that? It's a journey – and nothing short of a huge burden – but one that'll be all the sweeter when it's over. Plus, when you get pretty good at realising your partner's / friend's level of ability, "**Beth?**" soon becomes your greatest ally. Did your learner just ask or say something in English you know full well they can say in Welsh? "**Sori, beth?**" can be repeated as many times as you like until they realise you're waiting for them to give it a shot in Welsh. The additional '*+ smile*' can be applied here too, if you like.

Before writing this chapter, I put the following thought to my social media cronies on Twitter: "TIPS FOR WELSH SPEAKERS ON

HOW TO TEACH CYMRAEG TO NON-WELSH SPEAKERS. GO:" Amongst the waves of responses like 'introduce them to Welsh music,' 'be patient,' 'watch S4C with subtitles together,' 'encourage all the time' and even 'get drunk,' by far the most common responses from learners were pleas to not have native speakers switch back to English if they sensed a struggling learner. This struck a chord with me as a learner of multiple languages myself. I was once told by a French speaker that French people will often speak back in English just as an excuse to practise their own English skills. As selfish as this may seem, it's totally understandable, but it's not an excuse that native speakers can use here in Wales. There aren't many Welsh people who need to practise their English... although if some of the comments bemoaning the Welsh language on Twitter are anything by which to go, some people could do with working on their SPAG!

Just as I learned from my colleague in Coleg Cambria moments before my very first adult class, saying and doing as much as you can in your target language is key. Setting such an example is akin to how we learn as children in that it opens up the part of our mind where we store our Welsh. It's why multilingual children rarely mix up between different languages; linking places and occasions with the language(s) they use. I experienced this first-hand in my university days, be they in lectures or in my part time job. But this isn't to say that speaking nothing but Welsh to someone who's just told you they wish to learn is the way to go. Choose your situations. If you've just heard something on the TV or radio regarding a political mishap or a celebrity scandal, one can't expect a learner to be able to take in such vocabulary and sentence structures to discuss it without warning or prior preparation. I've got a degree and I don't think I could! This is where, once again, the burden is placed on the teacher. It's down to them to gauge situations and choose where to apply this technique. And, in the certainty of us teachers getting it wrong sometimes, an apology, admission or realisation (and encouragement to continue) will go a long way for your learner.

When faced with such a burden and various effort-consuming techniques, it's surprising that most speakers don't just end up turning away those who wish to learn the language from them straight away. The reason we don't? Because Welsh is worth it. At the end of the day, however, the age-old Welsh saying that there'll always be **tri chynnig i Gymro** (*three attempts for a Welshman*) may well be true, but for nervous non-speakers it can often be as fragile as one strike and they're out.

## OES RAID IDDI FARW?
*Must Welsh die?*

Imagine your great-grandchildren asking what '**Cymru**' means and you telling them it's the name of *Wales* in an old language people *used* to speak.

The truth is, you don't know what you've got until it's gone – an old cliché that can be applied to almost every situation in life and none more so than to monoglot English speakers in eastern areas of Wales. Around here, any time even fluent speakers hear Welsh in the wild from complete strangers it's a talking point. "**Ooo, ma' nhw'n siarad Cymraeg yne. Ŵrach 'den ni'n 'nabod nhw!**" – *They're speaking Welsh there. Maybe we know them!* Yep, it's super sad but I promise there's a Welsh speaker from eastern Wales who's read this and chuckled to themselves. There may well only be '**dipyn bach**' spoken around these parts, but there's heart and soul in each and every word – controversially perhaps more so than in conversations that happen in the western strongholds of the language. In each word of Welsh uttered in Clwyd or Cardiff, in Powys or Prestatyn, there is the bedrock for a brighter future. A reminder that the language lives in areas disregarded by many as having already lost it and therefore there's no point learning or using it here. What's more, there's an almost 'proud' tone, if one exists, when people use the Welsh they know around where I live. Sometimes it can be difficult for non-speakers to distinguish it from just a Welsh speaker patronisingly using the language – *"probably moaning about me straight to my face knowing I can't* *understand!*" etc etc etc. I can categorically confirm that simply isn't the case, by the way. I've got better things to talk about, **diolch yn fawr**. This tone is from a pride in knowing you're doing something for a language that needs a hand. I'm sure I speak for many when I say that the feeling of speaking Welsh in border areas is be a bit like being the tallest person in a group of people – it's not anyone's fault and isn't meant to upset anyone, but it still feels pretty cool anyway. It's a strange yet refreshing feeling and one that you want to have over and over again.

It does, however, beg the question that if it takes an area almost completely losing Welsh to make people feel the **calon** (*heart*) in knowing they're ultimately making a difference to it, does Welsh need to die *everywhere* in Wales in order to have that feeling return to the whole of the country? There remain large areas of Wales where Welsh is spoken just because that's what's done, not as an act of almost defiance in the face of a changing linguistic situation. Sadly, however, even numbers in these "Welsh Wales" areas are in decline. In these traditional western strongholds of the Welsh language, migration of non-speakers in and of native speakers out has led to rapid losses. As of 2011, Gwynedd was just 65% Welsh-speaking (down from 72% in 1991) and, more worryingly, Ceredigion's Welsh speaking numbers dropped below 50% in the same census for the first time since Welsh was initially spoken there well over a millennium ago. Now then, you present these statistics to speakers of other minority languages around the world and they'd tell us to stop our moaning; their own languages declining at much more alarming rates. But for Wales, in total opposite to Ireland who favoured political independence over their language, we still choose to prioritise linguistic independence over political; a prioritising of a language like hardly anywhere else in the world.

Ask some people and they'll tell you Welsh died in eastern border regions at the same time it died in Shropshire, Cheshire and Herefordshire etc. When you check out maps, there are many areas in the aforementioned shires with more Welsh place-names than in parts of Flintshire, Wrexham and Powys. With some exceptions, the rule of thumb is that the further east you travel, the less Welsh is heard. Howsoever damning and saddening the statistics can be for my own Flintshire (lower than 10% in some places), I still live in hope. Well, actually I live in Abermor-ddu; around 1 mile from the village of Hope, but I did go to school there. I digress. I still live in hope that it's here where Welsh is fought for and argued for; where Welsh is used not only as a medium of conversation, but as a resistance to maintaining the memory of people revered in these parts for millennia. The rabid flames of Welsh may have been all but extinguished here, yet the ashes still harbour poignant embers. Again, it begs the question; does a language need to hit rock bottom to be reminded of its importance? Today, according to numerous studies, the greatest number of requests for Welsh-medium education are in eastern Wales and, even more interestingly, the actual numbers of Welsh speakers in these borderlands is showing the opposite to the declining trends of those in the west. Here, the old language is growing. The vast *numbers* of speakers remain in the west while the swinging pendulum of *percentages* favours the east. Our tiny breaths of spoken Welsh upon those glowing embers are reigniting our hearths.

## SIARAD CYMRAEG NEU JYST SIARAD?
### *Speaking Welsh or just speaking?*

The fact that Welsh is not considered extinct is, for me, because there are still plenty of people out there who use it 'unconsciously.' They don't care whether they're speaking Welsh, German, Catalan or Sesotho; they just *speak*. There's no thought of how using Welsh so readily ensures its survival, it's just used as it has been since the days of Brutus [sic]. In my opinion, it's largely down to this 'arrogance' – for want of a better word – that ensures the survival of Welsh.

Don't think for one second that this only applies to a bunch of elderly people in tiny villages on the west coast either. Go to most western towns and the youngsters are using it just as freely. I once saw a sign in Y Bala that read '**Dim parcio ar unrhyw adeg**' (*No parking at any time*) graffitied to later read '**Parcio am rhyw**' (*Parking for sex*). Unsurprisingly, I chose to giggle loudly rather than take issue with the fact that the preposition '**am**' should've caused a soft mutation on the word '**rhyw**.' It's also really difficult to condemn the mutilation of public signage in this instance too! I'm happy to bet good money that this graffiti wasn't done by a cheeky geriatric on his daily stroll.

Regardless of age, the truth is that if a language has come to you naturally, you'll just use it. It's in your blood. Languages need this arrogance. It's also the best comeback to those who claim Welsh is but a "*hobby language*." Conversely, if a language comes to you because you felt a desire to learn it, the feelings are different. As someone who gained fluency later in life, I have days where I go to bed and lie down realising how I can't recall speaking (or even thinking) an entire word of English that day. The point here is that, because I learnt Welsh, I'm aware of it – even if only afterwards. It doesn't pain me, but I do find it a bit of a shame I'll probably never *not* be conscious of the language I use.

In many ways, Wales is linguistically split into three parts; non-Welsh-speakers, native Welsh speakers who just 'use it', and Welsh speakers who consciously choose to use it because they know they must. Surely that's not too a healthy situation for a nation of 3.6 million, but who's correct here? Should we all just speak English? Should we just let the numbers of native speakers dwindle without adding learners until it fades into a language that people *used* to hear old folk speak? Or do we continue in the potentially never-ending fight to make more speakers less aware of the language they use? Were the answers easy, we'd have done something about it already. It's as simple (or not) as that.

*****

If we wish to reinstate Welsh and have residents and visitors alike realise its place in a modern Wales, we have to use it ourselves. Set an example. In as much as I aim throughout these pages to motivate learners into using their language, those of us already fluent in the language have just as big a part to play – if not bigger. I'm not a fan of the term 'normalise,' but my brain lacks an appropriate synonym to express how the simple act of ensuring we all use what we know can do wonders for how people view the Welsh language. The truth is, no matter where in Wales we are – native stronghold or otherwise – if every single fluent speaker started every conversation in Welsh and ended it with a **diolch** or a **hwyl fawr**, non-speakers would be far less inclined to try and pass off not using their own skills with the excuse that "it's a dying language."

Remember Phil Lovell, the guy who tutored me during my teacher training placement in Rhosllannerchrugog? Well we stayed in contact over the years and, in 2018, along with a former teacher from my Castell Alun high school days, Gareth Lloyd, I was invited to take part in the pair's new Welsh-language radio show broadcast on Wrexham's *Calon FM*. **Hwntw a'r Gog** (the Southerner and the Northerner) featured Welsh music, discussion, interviews and general joking around on an otherwise monoglot English station. My invitation was not to be an inspiring guest speaker, to discuss an important local topic, or even to play a song on my old acoustic guitar. My job was to go out into the wild and, armed with only a dictaphone and a fiver, attempt to order fast food somewhere in the Wrexham area using only Welsh.

My victim was a guy called Chris who later told me he'd been on Saturday night TV recently and so he was no stranger to being put on the spot by the media. In truth, I did pre-warn him about my challenge and asked for his permission etc before we started, but after that he jumped right in. Admitting to having forgotten much of the Welsh he learned at school, I managed to order my favourite Subway sandwich completely in Welsh. There was a bit of pointing at times and Chris asked me various questions in English, but he was totally undeterred when I used nothing but Welsh with him. He even chucked a **croeso** at the end when I thanked him. As I left, the woman in the queue before me admitted she understood very little of the conversation but still managed to get her voice onto the clip by shouting '**bendigedig**' just before I pressed the stop button. **Bendigedig** indeed!

Aside from the fun element of doing such a thing for Phil and Gareth's show, my hypothesis that I'd get by just fine ordering a meticulously personalised sandwich of my choice in the medium of the language of my choice was proved right. I hope there's a message in there other than that Subway's butties are well nice.

# PENNOD 5
# AMDDIFFYN EIN CYMRAEG – Defending our Welsh

## CADW'R FFYDD
*Keeping the faith*

As I've said before, language shapes our reality – it's simply *that* important. Important enough even for some to knock on people's doors and hand out fliers about it. However, there's plenty of preaching in life without someone moulding Welsh into a new religion.

Growing up, identifying with a religion was about as important to me as were politics, responsibilities, and mortgages; *id est*, not at all. I was never christened and never set foot in a church until my *nain* passed away in 1998. The only ways religion touched my life were the songs we sang in primary school assemblies and the prayers we said before dinner time. Looking back now as a teacher myself, I understand many of these instances were only encouraged by our teachers because they were professionally obliged to do so anyway. As I grew into my teens, religion became only something I understood to be the primary cause of the world's disagreements before I finally realised that it was actually largely just human greed. The only time I ever even slightly considered religion to be of use was one lad's determination in high school that being spotted by teachers saying the Lord's Prayer during assembly meant you didn't get shouted at as much in lessons. Quite the claim.

My disassociation with religion continues to this day. I'm in no way against someone having a faith as I know that many find solace and harmony in it, but I guess I'm yet to appreciate that side of it myself, while my ever-sceptical mind ensures that I probably never will. Perhaps that's sad, but I can at least say I find faith and solitude via other means.

Occasionally, in fact, I 'pity' religion and attempts by its followers to encourage others unto it – particularly Christianity seeing as that's the primary faith of those around whom I live, even though I'm sure all the world's religions and faiths struggle to find new blood to carry their flame into an uncertain future. I pity it because, for me at least, its determined and moral-abiding followers are fighting what I perceive to be a losing battle. It's certainly no secret that more and more people are either turning their backs on religion completely or are simply too busy to find a place for it in their fast-paced, modern lives. I don't at all doubt that it must be difficult to remain relevant in this modern world. Often I'll notice small chapels and churches offering youth-friendly gatherings to encourage youngsters to faith. On many occasions, I find myself wanting to place my slowly shaking head in my hands at the sight of said events and advertisements; all the time realising that their recruitment techniques have reduced themselves to not much more than mere pitiful gimmickry. I see the same with some political parties too. Stop trying so hard!

But that's the Catch-22. To remain relevant, religions must fight in any way they can to maintain their purpose. No longer is the promise of 'heaven' and the warning of 'hell' enough to turn non-believers into regular churchgoers. I suppose science and its numerous research-based answers to questions previously too perilous to even consider has deemed faith nothing more than irrelevant to many. It's sad, certainly, but it's reality.

As a teacher of a language creeping up on two millennia in age, I am constantly aching to share with students why *I* know the Welsh language is relevant. However, over the past ten-or-so years of being a teacher, it often surprisingly pained me to hear students say they enjoy my lessons. It pained me to think that, despite the fact they're leaving my classroom with more knowledge of our national language than when they walked in, they might primarily enjoy my gimmicky PowerPoint presentations and quirky, yet often cringy, vocab' videos. Learning Welsh might, for them, merely be a side effect in an otherwise fun way to spend an hour behind a desk. Is that how I want Welsh to be perceived? Wonderful examination results year on year fill me with genuine pride in each and every student but I worry as to whether their minds, fully loaded with vocabulary and phrases as ammunition, are brave enough to actually then use their acquired skills in the real world or whether it was all for nothing. I think of students past and remind myself of their abilities in lessons – knowing their standard of Welsh was far better than mine when I was at their age. I went on to learn it, but will *they* eventually bridge the gap between realising they possess the knowledge and having the guts to step into daily-use competency? Do students yearn for trips to the Urdd camps at Glan-llyn or Llangrannog to practise their Welsh, or just to get away from their parents for a weekend and spend time with their mates? Do adults scramble to find local Welsh classes to arm themselves with the tools to ask for a pint of Wrexham Lager at their local watering hole in Welsh or simply to jazz up their CVs?

It's no secret that those attempting to promote and encourage the Welsh language work tirelessly to get our nation conversing in Welsh. There is certainly no shortage of events all over this land offering opportunities to experience the language. But what if we too are trying too hard? I once went to an evening organised by a college for their learners and around 40% of those attending were tutors. What if our attempts to encourage Wales' native tongue are the final gasps of a community spirit that has no place in an evolving world? What place, if any, will Welsh have in years to come?

When I see chapels opening their doors to young people with the hope of turning their heads to faith, deep down even my science-ridden outlook tells me those attending are there only to take selfies with friends and organise their weekend outing to McDonald's and Starbucks. I sometimes also consider how the rôle of education in incorporating religion into children's everyday lives has had only a detrimental effect (simply by, perhaps, trying too hard) in its attempts to embed itself into commonplace. I worry that, as a schooled subject rather than a natural and common phenomenon, Welsh has become much like religion; on a one-way road to oblivion. My mind forces me to question whether my life-choice of replacing the word *'thanks'* with **'diolch'** in every situation has, in the eyes of those who hear it, reduced itself to a mere gimmick – much like people of faith willing God's blessing upon non-believers. And there again appears our Catch-22. Were we [those 'burdened' with encouraging the use of Welsh] to refuse to 'sink' to levels of gimmickry then perhaps our language might not endure? Yet, at the same time, were we not to at least make an attempt to remain relevant via gimmickry and fun, would our goal of a bilingual populous become merely an unachievable dream? Like science has indirectly turned the masses away from religion with its wondrous explanations of our cosmos and everything in it, so too has the English language with all its free-flowing ease and global appeal turned the tides of speech against Welsh.

\*\*\*\*

Links between minority languages and various faiths do not end there. In 1567, William Salesbury, a prominent Welsh scholar, took it upon himself to translate the New Testament into Welsh. Salesbury had been inspired by the belief of Erasmus and Luther that the Bible should be available to all in their native tongue imploring; "**Mynwch yr yscrythur lan yn ych iaith**" – Demand *Holy Scripture in your language*. That's Late Middle Welsh, by the way, so don't worry if it looks a tad odd!
Okay, so his work ended up being not much more than a dialect-ridden attempt at a basic translation, but it was a start. Not only did Welsh people now have a religion they could actually understand (as opposed to the Latin or English they were forced to sit through every Sunday morning), but it proved that the good old Welsh desire to be at the cutting edge of change was

alive. By 1588 the Bishop William Morgan, with the help of Salesbury, took to the Greek, Latin and Hebrew versions of the Bible (Salesbury had only used the already translated English version) in search of a formality worthy of their god. At the same time (yet unbeknown to him), Morgan was standardising early modern Welsh.

It was on the demand of Elizabeth I (significantly the daughter of Henry VIII about whom I'll speak later) that the Bible was formally commissioned to be made available in Welsh under Morgan's guidance. But before we all rush to royalism, it's entirely plausible (and probably pretty much fact) that Elizabeth only encouraged the translation so as to ensure the million-or-so Welsh speakers of the time were fully behind her – both in religion and in homage. Even so, a desire to maintain a native language often inspires a desire for political independence and generates a spirit of rebellion – something many Irish residents of Fron-goch's POW camp near Y Bala knew all too well at the turn of the twentieth century. Back in the sixteenth century Elizabeth clearly knew this too, but her gamble paid off. Wales kept its language but conformed to its neighbour's choice of religion and, subsequently, to its laws and customs.

****

So, as to stand in solidarity with others in their struggle to endure the tests of a modern world, I shall lower my guard against religion and faith, and bid upon all the blessing of whomsoever your god(s) may be and pray to them that Welsh will, forever and ever, be a part of the fabric of our divine land. Our language clearly owes so much to religion having played a huge part in the protection and continuation of Welsh. It's no secret that without the support of the church – even into the early 20th century where the only Welsh-medium education available was via Sunday Schools while public schools were actively discouraging its use – the Welsh language would have ceased to exist.

Wales is, after all, God's own country and the Welsh language itself, **iaith y nefoedd** – *the language of the heaven*s.

# BRENIN Y BRATIAU
## *Royally screwed*

Henry VIII, known in the native language of his paternal ancestors as *Harri'r 8$^{fed}$*, ascended the throne of England in 1509 after the death of his Pembroke-born father, Harri Tudur aka Henry VII of England. Were it not for Harri Tudur and the aid of the people of his native land (and some Bretons from whence he'd been exiled for twelve years), it's unlikely the House of Tudor would have ever sat on the throne of England and, subsequently, would have meant Henry VIII and his six wives (as well as Protestantism and monastery dissolution) would never have happened. The Tudor dynasty certainly wouldn't have received the airtime it currently commands in school history lessons throughout these islands.

It's a little-known fact outside of Wales that Henry VIII's almost fascist attitude of 'one nation, one language' was one of the primary reasons behind what became a dislike and distrust of the Welsh language amongst the common folk – something that, arguably, continues to this very day. Despite his strong Welsh heritage, Henry VIII's Laws in Wales Acts of 1535 and 1542 not only saw Wales legally annexed as part of England, but imposed damning restrictions on the people of Wales stating that; *"Some rude and ignorant People have made Distinction and Diversity between the King's Subjects of this Realm, and his Subjects of the said Dominion and Principality [sic] of* Wales. *Notice and Knowledge of his Laws of this Realm, and utterly to extirp all and singular the sinister Usages and Customs differing* from the same, and to bring the said Subjects of this his Realm, and of his said Dominion of Wales, to an amicable Concord and Unity... That his said Country or Dominion of Wales shall be, stand and continue for ever from henceforth incorporated, united and annexed to and with this his Realm of England." Essentially, the Welsh were too different to their neighbours and Henry didn't like it. Henry's use of words like *'rude,' 'ignorant'* and *'sinister'* still raise their heads in modern-day Wales at times too; half a millennium later.

With regards specifically to the language, dignity in Henry's realm was afforded only to those who denounced their linguistic heritage; *"People of the same Dominion [Wales] have and do daily use a speche nothing like, ne consonant to the natural Mother Tongue used within this Realm [England], [...] all and singular Person and Persons, born and to be born in the said Principality Dominion or Country of Wales, shall have enjoy and inherit all and singular Freedoms Liberties Rights Privileges and Laws within this his Realm, and the King's other Dominions, as other the King's Subjects naturally born within the same have enjoy and inherit."* Finally, Section 20 of the 1535 Act made English the sole language of the law courts and stated that those who used Welsh would not be appointed to, or paid for, any public office in Wales; *"No Person or Persons that use the Welch Speech or Language, shall have or enjoy any manner Office or Fees within this Realm of England, Wales, or other the King's Dominion, upon Pain of forfeiting the same Offices or Fees, unless he or they use and exercise the English Speech or*

*Language.*" It's also worth pointing out that these Acts and their contents remained enshrined in law in Wales until 1967!

It wasn't just Welsh that experienced a turbulent Middle Ages either. The 1366 Statutes of Kilkenny politicised the Irish language as an act of 'disloyalty' stating *"If any English or Irish living among the English use the Irish language amongst themselves [...] and thereof be attained, his lands and tenements, if he have any, shall be seized into the hands of his immediate Lord."* Not satisfied with his plans to eradicate only the Welsh language, Henry VIII once again waded in with an instruction to his colonial rulers in Gaillimh (*Galway*), Ireland in 1536 ordering that *"every inhabitant within said town endeavor themselves to speak English."* A further statute issued the following year blamed the Irish people's attachment to their language as the primary cause of their *"certain savage and wild kind and manner of living."*

The dissolution of monasteries (signed off by, you guessed it, Henry VIII) had an extremely damning indirect effect on the Cornish language too as the overhaul of Catholicism into Protestantism wounded Cornish-speaking Christians. In his article for the Journal of British Studies in 1999 entitled '*The dissidence of despair: rebellion and identity in early modern Cornwall,*' Mark Stoyle explained how the Catholic Church had *"proved itself extremely accommodating of Cornish language and culture."* Under Henry VIII, that support was in tatters and it only took around 200 years to batter Cornish until the last monoglot Cornish speaker, Dolly Pentreath, died in 1777. Around the same time Cornish was fizzling out, the

*Gàidhealtachd* (the Gaelic-speaking Highlands of Scotland) was being cleared out between 1750 and 1860 by British landowners for more farmland. This displaced vast swathes of Gaelic communities with many emigrating as far away as Canada where small, Gaelic-speaking communities still endure the modern-day pressures of the English language on the other side of the Atlantic Ocean. Over in continental Europe, school walls across Brittany, the Basque Country and northern Catalonia were adorned with the French phrase *'Parlez français – Soyez propres'* (Speak French – Be clean). This phrase can still be heard today directed at speakers of anything other than French.

Over time, a connection was established in the psyche of the masses between being a 'wild savage' and having the ability to speak the native languages of the British Isles; Cornish in Cornwall, Manx on the Isle of Man, Gaelic in Scotland, Irish in Ireland and Welsh in Wales. These tactics to discourage the use of anything other than English – due to the initial failure in trying to eradicate the native tongues completely – continued across centuries. *'The Necessity for De-Anglicising Ireland'* written in November 1892 by Irish scholar, poet, politician, and founder of the Gaelic League, Douglas Hyde, explains that the people of Ireland *"ceased to be Irish without becoming English."* This phrase is not uncommon amongst the people of Ireland today and is one that's all too easy to appropriate to ourselves in Wales. From the days of Edward I and his imposing castle-towns across the north and west, the Welsh language became associated less with wealth and more with want – a trend that continued well into the early 20th century.

But in the same way that it took 600 years to reduce the percentage of Welsh speakers from around 95% to 25% through playing on the misconception of want over wealth, so too must we, as those who wish to see the language reinstated, prepare for a lengthy road to reversing this shift and reverting the language back into every corner of our nation. It's perhaps also worth noting here that, with the Welsh Government's recent emphasis on ensuring the survival of the language, more and more people that some might describe as 'middle class' are learning, using and passing on the language whereas 'working class' communities across Wales seem to prefer English. Funny, that.

Blame the fact we've only had a truly separate education system to our neighbours next door since 2017, but centuries of tyrannical battery has turned Wales from being one of the most classically learned and cultured nations in Europe to what is now, according to Pisa (the Programme for International Student Assessment), one of the least well-educated. A people so accustomed to prioritising the arts and education portrayed as savages and backwards in mainstream psyches and media – if portrayed at all. This is what we're up against.

# CEFNDRYD CELTAIDD
*Celtic cousins*

You may have noticed that I've referenced many of the Celtic nations and their languages throughout this book – a trend which is about to continue in this section. It's not just down to my love for – and constant attempts to learn – their beautiful languages that I include them so often, but for the fact that each of the six living Celtic languages has witnessed decline to different degrees of severity over the last few centuries, but always with a very similar reason for said decline.

In the first meeting of *Yn Cheshaght Ghailckach* (The Manx Language Society) in March 1899, William Quayle said; *"When a nation loses its language, it loses its more precious heritage; it loses its patriotism; it loses its nationality, and becomes, as it were, a nation dwelling in a strange land."* The following popular Welsh saying epitomises these thoughts perfectly: **Cenedl heb iaith, cenedl heb galon** (*A nation without a language is a nation without a heart*). To the Cornish, **Den heb tavas a gollas y dir** (*a man without a language loses his nation*) with the Bretons too placing their language at the heart of their national pride; **Heb brezhoneg, Breizh ebet** (*Without Breton, Brittany is nothing*). Manx (**Çheer gyn çhengey, çheer gyn ennym**) and Scots Gaelic (**Tìr gun chànan, tìr gun anam**) both mirror the Irish phrase; **"Tír gan teanga, tír gan anam"** – *A nation without a language is a nation without a soul."*

Phrases, sayings, and idioms are littered throughout so many minority languages that recognise the need to maintain our dialects. Turning back to our own language and I implore anyone to find me a more rousing chorus of a more rousing national anthem in the world:

> **"Gwlad, gwlad, pleidiol wyf i'm gwlad. /**
> **Tra môr yn fur i'r bur hoff bau, /**
> **O bydded i'r hen iaith barhau."**
> *"Nation, nation, I'm devoted to my nation. /*
> *While the sea is a wall to this fair, favoured land, /*
> *Oh the old language shall endure."*

Yet even amidst these cries of defiance, there is an important message we can all take. The notion that speaking Welsh makes them 'more Welsh' as a result exists largely in the imagination of people who imagine that others are constantly judging them. With hindsight, I think my own desire to learn was based fundamentally on the fact I believed I wasn't truly Welsh until I'd mastered our native language. When I speak to people these days who believe in a similar moral, I tell them that being Welsh is a state of mind, regardless of their language skills. I always add, however, that with so much of our culture and heritage locked in our language, giving Welsh a good shot will never harm your Welshness.

# GADEWCH IDDYNT EU HIAITH; DIM OND EI CHANU Y MAENT
*Give them their language; all they do with it is sing*

With responsibilities for Welsh across the curriculum in the school in which I work, I'm charged with ensuring that we are doing the best we can to ensure Welsh has an incidental yet natural place in students' everyday lives. In addition to putting on Welsh-themed events and ensuring the school has an obvious Welsh ethos, I've put on regular sessions for staff wishing to squeeze more Welsh into their lessons, as well as improving their own skills personally too.

The tables have long since turned from the days of Coventry MP, William Williams' proposal that *"an Inquiry be made into the state of Education in the Principality [sic] of Wales"* that led to the infamous **Brad y Llyfrau Gleision** – *the Treachery of the Blue Books*. 1847 saw three non Welsh-speaking commissioners from England visit schools in Wales and eventually publish a triple-volume, blue-covered set of accounts and recommendations entitled *'Reports of the commissioners of enquiry into the state of education in Wales.'* The reports, hugely critical of the Welsh language as a medium of education, caused nothing short of uproar in Wales for disparaging not only the language, but also the people of Wales. One quotation from the reports claimed that Welsh was a *"barrier to moral progress and commercial prosperity"* in Wales.

The 'Welsh Not' was no doubt an obvious contributor, but it cannot be denied that the remarks made in the Blue Books represented a huge reason behind so many parents in Wales discouraging their own use of Welsh with their children. Responses to the reports from the Church of England and The Times newspaper (respectively) screamed arrogance but still further fuelled the fires of immorality surrounding the ability to speak Welsh; *"The Welsh language is a vast drawback to Wales and a manifold barrier to the moral progress and commercial prosperity of the people." "Its [the Welsh language] prevalence and the ignorance of English have excluded and even now exclude the Welsh people from the civilisation of their English neighbours. An Eisteddfod [...] is simply a foolish interference with the natural progress of civilisation and prosperity."*

Even the BBC during the early part of the last century actively discouraged the use of the native languages. The British Broadcasting Corporation has certainly come a long way since all but condemning the native languages of these islands, but back in 1927 as a response to demands to allow Welsh to be broadcast on the radio, E R Appleton, the BBC's 'Director of the Western Region,' all but declared the native Celtic languages of these islands a curse on the people; *"To use the ancient languages regularly – Welsh, Irish, Gaelic and Manx – [...] would be to either serve propaganda purposes or to disregard the needs of the greatest number in the interests of those who use the languages for aesthetic and sentimental reasons rather than for practical purposes."* He went on to say that were the Welsh to *"get their way, the official language [English] would lose its grip."*

Nowadays, as calls to devolve broadcasting are strengthened, many believe the BBC are using Welsh TV License taxes unfairly.

Some say that if 20% of Wales can speak Welsh, BBC Cymru|Wales (and other media outlets) should be at least providing a fifth of all their content in Welsh. The BBC has also been accused of lowering the language to all but tokenism after numerous occasions of seemingly expecting Welsh speakers to be satisfied when one of our songs is heard as background music by UK-wide audiences once every few years. An article in August 2011 by the Daily Post, Trinity Mirror's media arm in north Wales, seemed to fall for this hook, line and sinker; *"A BAND will receive exposure that many artists could only dream of after being chosen as the title song for Football Focus. Last Saturday saw* UnDegPedwar *by* y Niwl*, chosen as the intro music for the long-running BBC One programme."*

Our music is powerful. When we sing, we open the very soul of ourselves and of our languages; every lyric bringing a lifeblood. We relate to an ancient, motherly belonging. The warm air of our language in full voice. Sung with passion. Laced with dance and laughter. We are known as the land of song for a reason. Songs and rhymes are the first things we learn as children and we remember them for the rest of our lives, as proved in 2020 by 96-year-old Ray McDermott. Ray had moved to the United States from Carmarthenshire in her mid-20s and, until a social media plea from her son yielded hundreds of responses, had not spoken her native language since then. Various videos emerged of Ray singing songs of her childhood explaining how the chance to share her songs again *"actually brought tears to my eyes."*

Music defends us and it keeps our culture safe. The message of Wales' song is that one may do with us what they will politically, but the fate of our language (and therefore our culture) is for our deciding and ours alone. In a 2014 article for the New York Times, American-born Bangor University Professor Jerry Hunter said; *"Once the Welsh lost their language, they lost their main identifier and assimilated."* He went on to describe how *"Welshness, more than any other national identity in Britain, relies on its linguistic and cultural legacy."* We can define ourselves as Welsh and/or proudly provide a full explanation to people in foreign lands of who we are (until someone inevitably must resort to saying the words *Gareth Bale* or *Geraint Thomas*). We can adore the Six Nations Rugby Championship and drape a dragon over our coffins when we die. The truth is that it doesn't matter. Were our hearts to no longer speak Welsh, that will have been the plan all along.

There will forever be those out there who believe the Welsh language to be a *"hindrance"* and a *"barrier to moral progress,"* but I promise you, wherever we go in the future as a Welsh nation, it's coming with us and we shall sing it forever.

## TROI AR EI BEN?
*Turned on its head?*

One might consider it a good thing that the likes of monarchies, centralised education systems and global media corporations have performed complete U-turns towards Welsh. Nowadays we hear of England's Prince Charles learning Welsh for a semester in Aberystwyth University, of Welsh Government education officials putting a huge emphasis on normalising the language in everyday school life, and of the BBC offering numerous sites, pages, and programming in Welsh – sometimes to global audiences. The cynic might then counter with claiming it's all too little too late that those who previously damned the language have finally realised that the will of the Welsh people was always to keep hold of their linguistic inheritance. Did these entities not simply employ the 'if you can't beat them, join them' idea and changed their mindset from out-and-out attempts to destroy the language to support it but on their terms? Whatever the reason, in the eyes of so many speakers of other minority languages that are in danger of dying as a mode of oral communication within the next 100 years, Welsh is a beacon of success. We are a shining light that minority languages have a future in a rapidly changing world.

Defending our language has become part and parcel of being a Welsh speaker. With the boom of social media there's now an open platform for adverse comments showing that displeasure towards the words we choose to express ourselves has not subsided amongst much of the common folk. One can argue that attacks on Welsh are simply a modern representation of the damning words of Henry VIII's laws and the treacherous Blue Books in the 19th century. Social media has created the perfect platform for people to disrespect the Welsh language whilst cowardly hiding behind a keyboard. It's become all too clear in recent years that anti-Welsh sentiment is as strong as it always was; except now it gets social airtime. Honestly, we should do our best to not get drawn in by it; **pawb at ei beth a'i bo** (*to each their own*). My only concern is that joking and disrespect leads to hatred and anger; two things that spread quicker these days than happiness and love.

There are two types of people who speak poorly of Welsh – those who genuinely dislike the language for a particular reason (and I say again, **pawb at ei beth a'i bo**) and those who come across the language haphazardly and feel the need to spread ill of it for no other reason than to ruffle a few feathers from behind a screen. **Pawb at ei beth a'i bo** does not extend to them. I guess that if you wish to badmouth Welsh, fine, but when you share your displeasure on social media and then moan when you're challenged, it sounds to me like you need to buy yourself a mirror, hold it facing you at arm's length and give yourself five minutes. Do not think for one second that we won't do as we've been forced to do for centuries and defend our language to the hilt.

As Welsh speakers we've heard them all; *"Where are the vowels?"* (We have seven actually!); *"They just spit on people!"* (Have you ever heard Turkish or even some dialects of Spanish and German? Scouse English, even?!); *"Why do letters have to change?"* (What's more than one 'wife'?); *"It's distracting on road signs!"* (If you're distracted by bilingual road signs, you shouldn't be left unattended using a fork, never mind be allowed to get behind a steering wheel!); *"I'd rather money was spent on other things."* (Westminster spends more money per annum on stationary for MPs than it does on the Welsh language. Fact!); *"But it's a dying language though, i'nit?"* (Statistically, no it isn't. The only thing dying around here is our patience with your ignorance!).

The final one is by far the best because people who post this genuinely believe they've got an indefensible point; *"It's just not useful in today's world."* For me, it's best to remain vigilant in employing the word 'useful' when it comes to evaluating, well, anything really. That which is truly useful in the eyes of so many is what connects them to other people – this includes the languages they speak. Welsh is just as important to me (and to thousands of other people across the planet) as any of the world's other 7,000+ living languages are to their speakers. I demand nothing of Welsh, and it demands nothing of me. What's more, to dismiss a language on the basis that it has little economic value in the world is like dismissing a friend because they aren't offering you a job. It's madness. If you measure wealth in pounds and dollars, then perhaps Chinese or Punjab is the language for you. I have no problem with that, and I wish you all the best in your quest to learn them. That's just not for me. If, like me, you measure wealth in the ability to connect with those around you, all of a sudden Welsh doesn't seem that useless.

The most recent milestone to be reached is the Welsh government's target of a million Welsh speakers in Wales by 2050 – just shy of 1/3$^{rd}$ of the population within a generation. But Welsh doesn't just *need* speakers and it certainly doesn't need targets. It could stay with the 1,000,000 global speakers it currently has forever and would hence never come close to dying. Just like what I try to impart to my students in my classes, all Welsh truly asks of people towards it is **parch** (*respect*).

# CYMRU A'R BYD
## *Wales and the world*

As a young girl growing up the Spanish-occupied Basque Country, Karmele Errekatxo had to attend secret classes in a church cellar in Bilbao in order to learn her native yet forbidden language, *Euskara*. Now a teacher herself teaching through the medium of Basque, she is quoted as saying that *"Language is the identity of a place. If you take language from a place, it dies. The [Spanish] dictatorship knew that and wanted Euskara to disappear."*

A phrase I spotted when brushing up my Breton skills on ClozeMaster recently epitomised Karmele's thoughts further, stating; **"N'eo ket en ur vro e vezer o chom, met en ur yezh. Setu petra eo ur vammvro, netra ebet arall"** – *It is not in a country which we live, but in a language. That is your homeland, nothing else*. I later heard this phrase was originally attributed to a Romanian, but I can't seem to find whom. Either way, the message is clear.

The Chiapas peoples, as described after a visit to Mexico by Irish journalist and writer, Michael McCaughan, maintain their native language despite Spanish becoming their language of commerce. Their 300,000-strong population (about the same as Cardiff) stand by their own language based on a belief that, despite it being largely *useless* in trade with wider communities, it remains *"the thread that weaves the social fabric [and] the unbroken link for their ancestors."*

I noticed a similar attitude as part of my current school's link with Saint Saviour's High School in the western Lesotho town of Hlotse (with the *HL* pronounced like the notorious *LL* sound in Welsh. Cool, huh?). The mountain kingdom of the Basotho is an enclave totally surrounded by South Africa and is home to around five million people; all of whom can speak English – their language of commerce – as well as their native language, Sesotho – their everyday language. After I visited in February 2018 I returned to Wales laughing at how my own country was defined as a first-world country and theirs third-world. With all their culture and passion and spontaneous breaking into song and dance, it reminded me of all the unique, community-orientated intricacies that Wales has all but lost over the centuries. Do any children still ask for their *Calennig* these days? Have you seen a Mari Lwyd or a wren in a box lately? Google it. Culturally at the very least, we are the third-world country by this comparison.

Whilst over there I was invited to observe lessons at the school and the teachers put aside huge amounts of time just to ask me questions about Wales' culture and language. Mountainous, culturally rich, impromptu-singing similarities aside, the fact that both Wales and Lesotho shared an enduring native language in the face of years of pressure to speak English was just as intriguing for their young people as it was for their teachers. I got a few opportunities to teach some basic Welsh out there too. It's incredible to think there are a few young people in the southern reaches of Africa who can count to ten in Welsh. *Kea leboha.*

That same year I visited Iceland with my school's geography department. With a similar population to the Chiapas people of less than half a million, our guide, Björn Rùriksson, (who divided his time between being a tourist guide, photographer, pilot, story teller and all-round Icelandic legend) explained to me how the people of Iceland too hold on to their native language; recognising it as the closest remaining living Germanic language to the one the original Vikings spoke when they first arrived on the island. Pretty much every single person across the whole population boasts fluency in Norwegian, Danish and Swedish (as well as, but to a lesser extent, German and English), but none will be caught chatting to other locals in anything other than *Íslenska*. Before we left, and in exchange for him teaching me how to correctly pronounce the name of the volcano that brought northern and western Europe to a standstill for a week in 2010, *Eyjafjallajökull*, Björn had asked me to teach him how to say the name of a certain village on Ynys Môn so he could impress our students. When attempting to describe to him how to pronounce our *LL* sound in Welsh, he swiftly told me to move on and he ended up pronouncing Llanfairpwllgwyngyllgogerychwyrndrobwllllantisiliogogogoch like an absolute boss. Turns out, like Sesotho, Icelandic has the same *LL* sound too. *Takk fyrir*, Björn.

And so, from being a small child wondering why a chair needed another word for it, to growing up realising what this old language means to so many people, it's been quite the life-altering journey for me. Learning the Welsh language to the degree I have remains to this day my greatest and proudest academic and spiritual achievement. Dare I say it, that will always remain the case. It seems that I, like many others including the Chiapas peoples, the Basotho and the Icelanders, measure wealth in tradition and community, in friendship and in heritage. That's my choice. My choice is Welsh.

# PENNOD 6
## IAITH ARBENNIG – *A Special Language*

**ENAID**
*Soul*

*"The best moments in reading are when you come across something – a thought, a feeling, a way of looking at things – which you had thought special and peculiar to you. Now here it is, set down by someone else, a person you have never met, someone even who is long dead. And it is as if a hand has come out and taken yours."*

Alan Bennett's words on the pleasures of losing oneself in a good book, as quoted in The Sunday Times, perfectly summarise my thoughts when applying my Welsh skills. Especially early on after admitting fluency, using my newly acquired words felt a lot like this to me; every phrase linking me to a different way of looking at things. From transforming my image of jellyfish as a child as being a friendly, wobbly creature, to finally getting stung by one and realising just why people from the north west refer to them as '**c\*nt y môr.**' It's not all silliness, mind. These days one might hear '**Dw i'n nerfus**' to express that someone's nervous, but we also hear '**Dw i ar bigau'r drain!**' – *I'm on the tips of thorns*. Quite the image. Where someone in English might say that there's a hard task or strenuous work ahead, in Welsh we'd say '**mae talcen caled o'n blaenau**' – *there's a hardened forehead before us*; relating to miners needing to wear hard hats when working underground. One of my favourites is '**dod at ei

**goed'** – *to come to one's trees*. This phrase, meaning to come to one's senses, paints a picture of someone returning to nature to find their wisdom. Even words like '**methu**' (*to fail, failing*) are nowadays used by younger speakers to express *'cannot'* – provoking a much more positive and optimistic outlook on life, I reckon. It's much easier on the tongue than '**ddim yn gallu**', too. One is welcomed with a fresh way of reading situations when using Welsh. Languages truly offer a different lens through which to view the world around us.

In an essay on writing in Irish, Nuala Ní Dhomhnaill writes that *"Languages, with their unique and unrepeatable way of looking at the world, are as important for human beings as the preservation of the remaining tropical rainforests are for biological diversity."* There exists in a language a soul and, as 8th-9th century Roman Emperor Charlemagne had it; *"To have another language is to possess a second soul."*

Aside from the school-friendly cliché of *'two languages, twice the choice,'* it's the truth in the following philosophical quotations that offers Wales a glimmer of hope for her ancient, linguistic heritage. Here are a few that inspired, and continue to inspire, me on my various language journeys:

- *"One language sets you in a corridor for life. Two languages open every door along the way."* –Frank Smith
- *"The limits of my language are the limits of my world."* – Ludwig Wittgenstein

- *"Language is the road map of a culture. It tells you where its people come from and where they are going."* –Rita Mae Brown
- *"If you talk to a man in a language he understands, that goes to his head. If you talk to him in his own language, that goes to his heart."* –Nelson Mandela

In Wales we're blessed and lucky enough to have the perfect excuse on the tips of our tongues to lose ourselves in another language. Let's do it.

# FEL HYN MAE I FOD
*This is how it's supposed to be*

During a first-year seminar in the university, our group was asked whether Welsh-language songs and literature should be translated into English (and/or other languages). The immediate consensus was yes; all of us wanting the fantastic, artistic prowess of our nation accessible to the whole world. We were then challenged to consider whether the cliché, 'lost in translation' is a real thing. It got me thinking; why does hearing the national anthem bring me to tears when I hear it in Welsh, but an English translation does nothing to me. It became clear that, whether a language is inherited from those who went before us or learned without any real link to any Welsh community whatsoever, native languages represent one of the final remnants of what is going on in the souls of writers and artists when they use(d) their native tongue. The language we choose to use represents our minds communicating with the world around us, be that in our own minds, with our family and friends, or in our spiritual consciousness. Much like it's reckoned that humanity's very existence represents the consciousness of the whole universe attempting to understand itself, so the languages we (choose to) speak represent our own consciousness attempting to understand our own surroundings and existence. The Welsh-speaking druids at the turn of the first millennium recognised this for centuries prior to making their last stand in around 57CE. Who knows what wisdom perished with them as the Romans crossed the Menai onto Ynys Môn and slaughtered them all? From legends, astronomy and ideas, to stories, games and even jokes; a whole way of looking at our world was lost and forgotten that day.

Just like the Chiapas peoples, the Basotho and the Icelanders who realise that their native language holds the key to their spiritual wellbeing and the unhindered link to their ancestors, I'm beginning to feel that this connection to times gone by connects me less to the heroes of the Mabinogi or the leaders and princes of this land, and more to the storytellers themselves. Clearly it's not just a connection to ancestors, for languages have the power to bind us even today. I've set foot in Europe (obviously), Asia, North America, and Africa and not once, amongst the plethora of different voices I've experienced, have I ever uttered the words; *'Oh wow, they're speaking English over there.'* There are things that a global language simply cannot do and I'm reminded of all the occasions I've said **diolch** and sparked a chat with someone who went from being a stranger to a five-minute-friend simply because of the language we speak.

I'll end this section with the words of a screenshot from someone's notes app that did the rounds on social media a few years ago when Welsh was in the middle of yet another battle to justify its existence to a bunch of monolingual, bigoted keyboard warriors. Unfortunately, I can't remember the attribution so if the author eventually reads this, get in touch with me and I'll make sure you're justly attributed when this book sells millions of copies and inevitably goes to print for a second time. *"I speak Welsh because my forefathers spoke the oldest language in Europe [sic]. Passed on without malice, agenda, 'political reasons' or even much thought. To be 'awkward'? To get 'better jobs?' To have the 'skill' of another language? To enrage an English person on holiday when they walk into 'that pub'? NO. We do it because it is as natural as breathing. It is part of our entire entity. Why the language of our forefathers 'offends' some, is a 'nuisance' to others and makes some feel 'uncomfortable' is a mystery to me. We speak Welsh. Always have, always will and you can be pretty damn sure our children will too."*

# PAM WYT TI'N CASÁU SAESNEG?
## *Why do you hate English?*

Wearing my Welsh-language heart on my sleeve has brought with it some interesting conversations. Believe it or not, I've been asked (on more than one occasion) why I hate the English language. Yep, I giggled too!

Allow me to straighten the record. The English language is awesome. I challenge anyone to sift through the world's 7,000 living languages and find one as versatile and as slick as English. Chaucer, Tolkien, Rowling, Wordsworth, and Shakespeare; these names are synonymous with the intense beauty that can be formed with the words of the English language. Argue that Shakespeare was a plagiarist with some of his works (was King Lear based on *Brenin Llŷr* of Celtic mythology fame?) but what he did with his words was immense – so much so that students in England and across the globe (pun totally intended) still study them today. It's claimed that Shakespeare, in order to put his messages across so successfully, simply *invented* new words. Of his 37 plays and five poetry collections, Shakespeare used around 17,500 words; around 10 percent of them were either dialectal terms or even just made entirely of his own invention. Words like *gossip*, *worthless* and *majestic* were either coined or adapted and given new meaning by Shakespeare himself. If that doesn't show the versatility of English, I don't know what else will.

As much as I'm not the biggest fan of his material, comedian Michael McIntyre once joked that one could choose pretty much any word in the English language and, so long as the context was sound, it could imply the word *'drunk.'* His joke concluded with something along the lines of "*... and I was totally gazeeboed!*" (How would one even spell that?)! The audience's laughter proved his point correct. But think about it, you simply can't say something like that in other languages. "*J'ai me gazeeboé!*" "*Ich habe mein gegazeeboen!*" "*Bhí mé i mo ghaisíbeoáil!*" "*Mi ges i fy nghasîboio!*" It just won't happen... tidily anyway!

Honestly, I'm proud to be able to speak English. At times I used to feel sad that my upbringing and education were not through the medium of Welsh but then, knowing both to complete fluency now, I'd much rather the path I've taken; partially because learning Welsh has made me live the whole experience of the language, but also because learning it was so much easier than I believe learning English would've been. As I mentioned earlier in the book, English has over a hundred irregular verbs; a great deal more than Welsh has. And these aren't even obscure verbs; they're common, everyday words that, as native English speakers, we simply take for granted.

And this is where I'll [finally] describe how I believe the English language has been 'highjacked.' Thank you for your patience since Chapter 4. Tin hats at the ready!

A regimented world works better when everyone speaks one language. Songs, media, games, life. One people speaking one language can be *controlled* far more easily. In Wales we've largely fallen into this trap. Watch my students' faces scrunch up when I tell them I read books in other languages and listen to Welsh bands. Most can't believe it. Despite changing the minds of many when I play songs by *Yws Gwynedd, Al Lewis* and *Alffa*, there will always be some who refuse to let themselves enjoy what they're hearing solely on the basis they don't understand the lyrics... unless it's *Gangnam Style* or, for more 'mature' readers, *Dragostea Din Tei* by Romanian dance-pop outfit, O-Zone. Perhaps this outlines a much wider problem amongst some young people and the sad truth behind why *Gwilym Bowen Rhys* will never headline Glastonbury.

As well as to possess a second soul and to open new doors, to speak another language is to straight up rebel. Our own language connects us to the roots of those who have gone before us; the roots of people who forged our home and called it such. We live and strive to be different – *rage, rage against the dying of the light*. How ironic to use the words of a Welshman whose opinions on the Welsh language were that our *"forefathers can keep it!"* and who denied any conscious use of the most famous and beautiful of all Welsh poetic metres, *cynghanedd*, in his writing even though his poetry is littered with it.

The language we choose to use shapes our outlook on life. As a language, English has been, and continues to be my preference when reading challenging texts about, well, anything. It just so happens that most of the stuff in which I find an interest has been written in English – a language I fully understand. I'm lucky. I know that. Despite this fact, there are some itches that English just can't scratch. For instance, there's stuff you can say in Welsh that you simply can't say in any other language. Take the chorus of Calon Lân;

> *A pure heart full of goodness /*
> *Fairer it is than the pretty lily /*
> *Only a pure heart can sing /*
> *Sing the day and sing the night.*

Give it a moment and, even in English, one can see the beauty in its words. Put a choir behind it *a cappella* and it's enough to make the hairs on the back of your neck stand up. And yet when I first heard Calon Lân as a self-confessed fluent Welsh speaker, I literally cried. Suddenly the beautiful words had context, even perhaps a consciousness. A simple song became a story which became a life. The Welsh language holds its riches close to its chest. It holds the keys to its own world of **harddwch** (*beauty*) that can only be unlocked by learning it. The language in which all its treasures were *meant* to be experienced is the key – from truly comprehending the minds of those who first documented the infamous King Arthur (not the Victorian version, of course), to experiencing the decay of a people's heritage and tradition laid out in such lexical dexterity where never before has such grief sounded so beautiful.

At the end of the day and in all honesty, no one enjoys a laugh as much as the Welsh. We'll happily take the slurs that we're only speaking Welsh to annoy non-speakers. The truth is we're proud of both our languages. It just so happens that we can appear to possess a chip on our shoulders when people cross the line. So back off, i'nit like!?!

# HWYL A SBRI
*Fun and more fun*

Different languages excel in different ways. Different intricacies, peculiarities and oddities are what make languages special. In addition, and something that gets linguists excited, many languages display acts of code-switching more than others. Some are amalgamations of many languages – of which many may now be considered extinct. Some possess idioms and sayings that paint the most wonderful pictures in one's mind – I once saw a Chinese sign asking people to not walk on a lawned area translated into English as that the *'tiny grass'* was *'sleeping.'*

Welsh would have to evolve quite significantly to be as versatile as English, but that doesn't mean Welsh doesn't have a few tricks up its sleeve. In the early days of Welsh, it was story telling where we excelled. The sacred triads of Welsh mythology and the introduction of heroes and celebrities – Merlin, Manawydan, Branwen, Rhiannon, Arthur. More recently, in the middle ages, poetry came to the fore and Welsh poetic metre became revered across the continent for its strict yet ever flowering means of turning sadness into beauty. But what of modern times?

When you gain a decent grasp on any language, it's amazing. But being able to discuss politics, gardening and the weather is a bit... well, boring, to be fair. Be honest, when you were younger and were presented with a dictionary in a different language, the first words you searched for were not 'economy,' 'philosopher' and 'computer.' I, at least, went straight for the naughty words. Every now and again you'd find a word like '*shit*' in a language dictionary and you'd feel like you'd won the lottery. They say it takes hearing/using a word 72 times to truly assimilate it into your vocabulary. When I learned what *merde* meant in French or *scheiße* in German, I probably said them 720 times on the first day! We crave fun, and finding humorous parts of languages keeps us going. It's like playing football for the first time where the bigger picture is having fun and being part of a team, but nothing quite beats the thrill of hearing a net's unique sound when you slam the ball into the top corner and overcome your opponents.

Speakers of Welsh are no different. Whereas in English-language media, the latest songs might be about love, partying and dancing, bands like *Gwibdaith Hen Frân* – who are still selling out gigs some 20 years since their first release – ensure their songs are full of humour and laughs. For example, the name of *Gwibdaith*'s second album was inspired by the phrase **'Tafod y Ddraig'** (*The Dragon's Tongue* – ie the Welsh language) but, with a sneaky play on words, went on sale in 2008 under the title **'Tafod dy Wraig'** (*Your Wife's Tongue)*! Make of that what you will.

Comedic short films online are proving hugely popular with youngsters and older folk alike. Commissioned by S4C after successes with shorter sketch programmes like *Dim Byd*, *Hansh* was created in 2017. In the words of its producers, Hansh is a **"Brathiad newydd bob dydd o bethau da: celf, comedi, cerddoriaeth, gemau, ffilmiau, teithio a phethau gwirion."** – a *new bite every day of good stuff: art, comedy, music, games, films, travel and stupid stuff."* To put its popularity into perspective, the service boasts 35,000 followers on Facebook and just shy of 10,000 each on their Twitter and Instagram platforms.

In addition to television, using the word 'Welsh' in the same sentence as the word 'technology' (without also using synonyms of 'pointless') is a conflict of terms in the eyes of many non-speakers. An oxymoron. A fallacy. As a 'dead language,' there can't be any provision for Welsh in the information age, right? Wrong! Not only is the Welsh language supported on platforms and operating systems like Microsoft Windows, Microsoft Office, Facebook, Twitter, Google et al, but the world of social media and real-time sharing is shaping the language and ensuring its survival. Just as I found when teaching Welsh, we can have fun with it. What's more, in a rapidly changing world with so much choice, I'm glad that Welsh has decided to cling to humour to bring us into the digital age.

# YN Y GÊM
*In the game*

Okay, so I wasn't totally honest with you earlier when I said that everyone in Iceland sticks to their language in the face of the claws of English. Whereas most people on the island recognised its importance, there was one occasion where I overheard a conversation in a Subway restaurant just outside Reykjavíc between a customer and a cashier. Two people; one ordering some grub, the other serving it. Both Icelanders. Both speaking *English*!

Björn, our Icelandic tour guide I mentioned earlier, was the first person to whom I spoke regarding my sadness and, in honesty, my surprise that two Icelanders would choose to speak English over their native tongue. It was then he informed me of something about which, as a Welshman, I was all too well versed; the damning of smaller languages by the many who choose to speak English before their native language(s). Björn was amazed to learn, considering Wales' proximity to the homeland of the world's *de facto* language, that Welsh had survived in the manner it had. I refused to inform him that my language boasted twice as many speakers as his own too!

We talked for hours about the situation of our respective languages as we passed some of the most beautiful landscapes on the planet until eventually, we began to consider how our languages might move forward. English amongst the Icelandic youth wasn't quite as ingrained as it is amongst Wales' young people, but a grave question remained; how might our languages maintain their relevance in a world rapidly losing its smaller languages at an alarming rate? The thing that struck me most from our conversation was how passionate Icelanders had, since the 90s, ensured that as many film producers and game developers as possible included Icelandic subtitles options on DVDs or as a playable language on video games. I guess the reason behind it was to ensure Icelandic maintained its relevance in the world – to ensure that the younger speakers didn't feel as though they had to learn Norwegian, German or English in order to enjoy the latest entertainment and media. Mainly down to our lack of sovereignty as a nation, Wales and the Welsh language were – and still are – totally overlooked when it comes to the gaming world. Even given that the population of the world's Icelandic speakers is less than the entire population of Wales' capital city, the fact that Iceland boasts its own seat at the United Nations means their language will always have a better chance than ours.

As you've probably guessed from this book, rarely a day goes by when I don't spend at least a few moments (but often much longer) every day thinking about how we could strengthen the Welsh language. I keep the faith that one day it will hit me and a simple idea will change our language's future for the better. Most of the time, however, I mainly despair in the knowledge that via drastic actions only we will save Welsh. John Saunders Lewis was indeed correct! But back in 2018 I had an idea, inspired by my chat with Björn, about that English conversation I overheard in Iceland. Unfortunately, it wasn't quite the linguistic silver bullet for which we've been searching but it at least linked two of my many passions — the preservation and expansion of the Welsh language and retro gaming!

I've been messing around with retro games, roms and emulators for years. Put simply, video games from the '80s and '90s are now downloadable to play on modern laptops and smartphones. Little chunks of childhood nostalgia squeezed together in 8-bit colourless harmony. Pokémon Red for the Nintendo GameBoy was one of my personal favourites as a kid and was one of the first games I remember that made me lose hundreds of hours and sap the juice of thousands of AA batteries. After (once again) playing and completing the game a few years ago — this time on my smartphone rather than a GameBoy that weighed a bloody ton — I needed a new challenge. A quick internet search led me to various articles on how the game's text could be edited. You'll never guess what I spent most of my 2018 summer doing!

Now a playable (and free to download) Welsh-language version of 1999's best-selling video game, I've been amazed by the support I've received for my summer-long efforts. I was even invited to do an interview for a group of Welsh speaking video game enthusiasts in mid-2020 about how the project came about. You can find clips on YouTube of the interview and of the game itself, as well as information on how to download it to play yourself on your smartphone or laptop.

Look, I'm under no illusions whatsoever that this project probably won't be the saviour of our native tongue like Morgan's Bible translation in 1588, but who knows? With a bit of luck, game developers might just take note of a surge in interest of gaming through the medium of Welsh and provide Welsh translations; much like the provision afforded to the numerous languages boasting far fewer speakers than Welsh has. At the very least it might afford a few hours of nostalgic fun to few 30-something-year-olds through the medium of their mother tongue. With the ability to work through the game and take in information at one's own pace, it might also turn out to be an additional resource to learners. Remembering from their youth what was initially presented in English might help learners to successfully work out what's being said in Welsh in a zero-pressure environment.

Finally, don't pity me. It was actually a lot of fun to do!

# AMDDIFFYN TAFODIAITH (RHAN 2)
*Defending dialect (Part 2)*

Thought I'd forgotten about Part 2, didn't you?!

Welsh speakers often bemoan the English language and blame the suffering of our own language on theirs, but I wish to go on record as one who refuses to accept the notion that the English (and French in the case of Breton) language has had as vast a detrimental effect on any of the native Celtic languages as many (wish to) believe. This is because we simply cannot be sure what potential linguistic gems were themselves displaced when the Celtic languages first inhabited our areas. For example, Pictish (probably a Celtic language itself) receded to extinction because of the influx of Gaelic (another Celtic language) in the north of modern-day Scotland. Some academics believe that there was a Brythonic language spoken on the Isle of Man before that to was displaced by Gaels and Vikings alike. To find annoyance in English (and other global languages) at the decline of the Celtic tongues is to be nothing short of a hypocrite in search for blame where there exists nothing but insecurity.

In December 2016, I attended a Christmas service in Mold's St Mary's Church led by Ysgol Maes Garmon – the town's Welsh-medium secondary school. It was genuinely a beautiful occasion filled with traditional Welsh songs performed exquisitely by the various choirs as well as some Welsh translations of some of my own favourite holiday tunes such as John Lennon's 'Merry Christmas (War is Over)' styled as '**Ryfel Beidia**.' Amazing.

There were festive readings from students of the school too. Readings from the Bible as well as more modern festive poems and verses. I remember, just after a reading, my wife (herself from western Wales) mention that the reader must have western parents due to a hint of a Gwynedd accent. After each reading, we noticed the same feature in most (if not all) students' accents. Could it be that both parents and teachers of these students were themselves from Gwynedd and therefore conversed only in their own, native dialects at school and/or at home? It begged the thought that maybe the only Welsh actually spoken in this area was by people originally from the western *Bro Gymraeg*. Were students conversing at home and in school in a dialect that was not native to eastern Wales? If this is the case, what hope for our dialect? Even thinking back to my dad's Welsh course (taught in Mold... though via Bangor University), I almost wept at how he ended up sounding more like a native of Caernarfon rather than a native of Leeswood.

As Welsh speakers, it almost seems subconscious that we must fashion ourselves as victims of the bully-language from over the border. We bemoan the influx of English which, in the view of many Welsh language enthusiasts, is squeezing the life out of the ancient tongue of the *Cymry*. This may well be the case, but rarely is a thought spared for the dialects bullied by larger ones within Welsh itself. For me it's just a bit sad how Welsh speakers moan that our language is under threat from the big, bad language next door when the same thing is happening with Welsh where larger dialects are threatening smaller ones.

It's clear that no school, no adult course nor even any online language course actually teaches our eastern linguistic peculiarities. Sure, there are a few online threads and discussion boards which mention our dialect, but I implore anyone to pick up a recent copy of *Papur Fama* or *Nene* (two local Welsh-language circulars from Mold and Rhosllannerchrugog respectively) and find me a cover-to-cover edition completely in our north-eastern dialect(s). Is *'Iaith Sir Fflint'* by Goronwy Wynne even still in print? When north eastern Welsh dies, we will all be to blame. And, what's more, my guess will be that we will comfort ourselves with "at least we still speak some form of Welsh" until the day comes when 'standard' Welsh itself dies.

It is true that finances afforded to the Welsh language leaves much to be desired. It is also true that languages and dialects themselves must evolve in order to survive. I cannot, however, accept the fact that lack of finance orders the death of a mode of conversation. I reluctantly stand by the view that a language must live on its own means – without depending on cash alone. Nor can I accept, despite understanding that they must adapt, that the act of dialects taken over and displaced by others of the same umbrella language can be honestly deemed as an evolution. To put it another way, the north-westernisation of north-eastern Welsh is not an evolution nor an adaptation but, in many ways, a suffocation.

As I've attempted to show throughout this chapter, my interest in languages is largely owed to a firm belief that the loss of a language is a loss of social connection and history. There lies in any way of speaking a way of living. A window on a locality which cannot be viewed through the glass of a new tongue. Would I rather a Flintshire 100% fluent in Gwyndodeg (north-western Welsh), or a Flintshire only 20% fluent but in its own dialect? I fear my answer is a selfish one. When north eastern Welsh dies, and die it will, we will lose the thoughts of Daniel Owen and ID Hooson, and the social intricacies of those who made this area what it is today. We will lose a piece of who we are. No one will eat **snapin** (*a snack*). No one will refer to the latest gadgets as **naci** (*handy, ie small but useful*). No one will **chwar'e'r hen** (*tell off, shout at;* literally. *to play the old*) with the naughty children. No one will even **nadu** (*cry*) over the loss of our dialect.

# IAITH Y NEFOEDD
## *The language of the heavens*

Unless the earthlings down at Nasa in the 1970s presumed that aliens conversed in **iaith y nefoedd**, someone obviously thought extremely highly of the Welsh language. On a golden record, amongst sounds of thunder and rain, nestled between a silhouette of a man and a woman, just below English and a Chinese dialect in a list of only 55 earthly tongues, on August 25th 2012, a recording of the following message entered interstellar space; "**Iechyd da i chwi yn awr ac yn oes oesoedd**" – *Good health to you now and forever more.* No words of the beautiful languages of Denmark, Catalonia nor Norway (nor a great many others for that matter) had a place on these eternal records. Someone thought very highly indeed of our homely inheritance.

It's believed that George Abbey, Seattle-born former director of the Johnson Space Center (whose family hailed from Sir Gaerfyrddin in south western Wales) may have had a positive effect on our ancient Celtic tongue's inclusion on both Voyager's golden records, but it's still pretty cool, mind. And since it's the only Celtic language on the records, I like to think that it represents all of Wales' Celtic cousins in an inter-stellar stand that demands 'Celtic peoples were here!' ... or 'Celtz woz ere' to any '90s graffiti fans!

But taking a step back from a floating concoction of metals and other materials, what can this mean for, not just Welsh, but for humanity? Voyager 1, which already requires more than two earth days to send a message to Nasa, receive one back, act upon it and send back confirmation of completion, will not last forever. By 2030, it will be impossible to power even a single unit on the probe. Inevitably, it will break down and it will decay – much like the planet from which it hails. Thankfully, the nature of the Golden Record ensures at least the important parts of Voyager's already continuous journey will endure the harshness of space. It will take another 40,000 years for whatever's left of Voyager 1 to reach our next closest star.

Now bear with me on this one. Imaginations at the ready! Let's presume there's no life out there capable of understanding the symbolic instructions required to play these everlasting sounds. Let's presume the Golden Record's contents will float around in space, keeping secret that which makes our planet personal to us. Meanwhile, a hurtling meteor wipes out all humanity on Earth. Yikes! Now imagine a new species (much like us humanoids who currently roam this lonely planet) evolves, much like we did, from the earliest life on Earth and make this rock – that will still possess the necessary cosmic requirements to harbour life – their home. Imagine the new humanoids, like us, get curious of their surroundings millions of years into their existence. Imagine they trawl the vastness inside and outside their galaxy. Imagine they find Voyager 1 (or 2) and its Golden Record. How about those greetings in 55 languages, as well as a collection of tiger sniffles and rabbit burps, are heard by a new species? A new humanity. These will be alien sounds from another time in space. Another people. Another world. And the language of the heavens – amidst a list of languages comprising but a fraction of our modes of human communication – will once again be heard on the spinning ball of rock it once called home. A gift of our everlasting existence.

Should humanity continue on this Earth for millennia more and Project Voyager becomes but a myth lost in the swathes of ancient Wikipedia pages about the pioneering event of the very first time humankind left their **milltir sgwâr** (*square mile / familiar surroundings*), people will speak of an ancient language of a people perhaps long gone. A language deemed important enough to be locked in time. A proof of an existence. And our descendants will hear it and they will learn of Welsh. "**Cymraeg am byth**," they'll whisper. *Welsh forever*.

# DIOLCH YN FAWR IAWN!

My first diolch goes to my family.

To my mother, my thanks are not for reading this book, but for letting Wales' skies be the first to meet my eyes after I was born – especially knowing she's a proud English woman. Well, not everyone can be perfect, right? I also owe her an even bigger diolch for teaching me to hold fast to my beliefs and my passions – no matter how niche and outspoken they may often be. Cheers, mam.

To my dad, diolch i ti hefyd. I like to think much of who I am today is down to you. You supported me throughout school and university, and even took your own plunge into learning this old language yourself. I hope you're even slightly as proud of me as I am of you.

And to the rest of my wonderful family and friends who support me without reservation and constantly stomach me turning absolutely anything back on Wales and its language; *"Oooh, doing some maths there, are we? Did you know the equals sign was first introduced by a Welshman?"* "Piss off, Stephen!"

I'm gwraig; diolch yn fawr iawn i tithau, heb os. Diolch am brawf-ddarllen a phrawf-ddarllen pob dim 'dwi 'di 'sgwennu. Mae'r angen am amynedd i fyw efo fi siŵr o fod wedi gorfod bod yn fwy'n ddiweddar wrth i fi daflu llwythi o syniadau a pharagraffau atat ti i ti bwyso a mesur. Dwi wir yn gwerthfawrogi pob eiliad – a dim jyst y rhai ti 'di treulio'n darllen hwn. 'Dwi'n dy garu di.

To my former teachers, lecturers, tutors, mentors, educators, and co-workers; diolch yn fawr. My love of Welsh may well have come about on its own accord, but it was your patience and belief in me that encouraged me to never stop working towards what I wanted.

Diolch to the two reasons this book came about. The first, the Women's Institute of Sychdyn who invited me to give a speech for Saint David's Day in 2019, the script for which became the ideas on which I built the rest of this book.
Secondly to Michael McCaughan whose book *'Coming Home: One Man's Return to the Irish Language'* (ISBN: 9780717171590, Publisher: Gill Books, Verdict: Well worth a read!) inspired me to share the story of my own journey of coming home to my own language. *Go raibh míle maith agaibh.*

Finally, diolch yn fawr iawn to you, the reader – unless, of course, you're reading this as one of the people I've already just thanked... I'm confused!
Throughout this book I've attempted to give Welsh a reason and a place in our ever-changing world. It's been a tough one to write because my world in Welsh is constantly evolving and new stories are written all the time. Take what you wish from these words and run with them, share them, dissect, and scrutinise them. The contents are as much yours as is the Welsh language itself.
This language offers you a new life in which to live where your own stories are ready to be written.

Even now after a degree in the Welsh language, as a teacher, a tutor, an annoying husband to a native speaker and the proud possessor of so many Welsh-speaking friends, I still feel different when I speak Welsh. In a crude way, I can only liken it to what I perceive a mild split-personality disorder to be. I feel different and act and express myself differently in Welsh. Much of the time I'm far less confident a person when speaking Welsh – all the time scrambling for the next word or sentence and worrying about whether my counterpart is understanding a bloody word I'm saying. Other times I feel one with my native land and the feelings I wish to express about it in English have so little value compared to when I say them in Welsh. It's a confusing, wonderful, anxious, and beautiful world when I use my Welsh and learning it represents, and will continue to represent until my final hour, my single greatest personal achievement.

So, you've just spent hours on end reading about everything to do with the Welsh language when said time could've been more efficiently spent actually bloody learning it. Along with all my gratitude to you for picking up this book, I also offer my belief that, armed with the thoughts and ideas herein, you'll be in better stead to face the challenges ahead – whichever stage you're at and whatever your relationship with the Welsh language. My hope is that hearing my story will cut a few corners in acquiring Welsh and prevent travelling too far down roads that might only lead to dead ends.

And remember, this language is yours and it is mine. Often your nemesis, but always your friend. So, do it. Learn it. Share it.

Better yourself and find yourself. By choosing to read these thoughts and ideas, you probably already possess the mindset that minority languages around the world crave so much; a respect for the underdog and a respect for heritage. If you've enjoyed reading this half as much as I've enjoyed putting it together then I'll rest easy. And, if I might be afforded the chance to proudly speak on behalf of our ancient language, **diolch yn fawr iawn i chi**.

Printed in Great Britain
by Amazon